Revelation:
The Last Call

MARY SMITH

WestBow
PRESS
A DIVISION OF THOMAS NELSON
& ZONDERVAN

Scripture taken from the *Amplified Bible*, Copyright © 1954, 1958, 1962, 1964, 1965, 1987 by The Lockman Foundation. Used by permission.

WestBow Press books may be ordered through booksellers or by contacting:

WestBow Press
A Division of Thomas Nelson & Zondervan
1663 Liberty Drive
Bloomington, IN 47403
www.westbowpress.com
1 (866) 928-1240

ISBN: 978-1-4908-5114-3 (sc)
ISBN: 978-1-4908-5113-6 (e)

Library of Congress Control Number: 2014916082

Printed in the United States of America.

WestBow Press rev. date: 09/18/2014

Contents

Preface vii

Introduction xi

Our World As It Was And Is 1

A Bit Of History 3

Jesus Comes To John With His Final Message 8

Jesus' Message To The Seven Churches 12

Jesus' Invitation Continues 17

Preparation Begins For The Final Victory 19

The Beginning Of The End 20

The Seventh Seal 30

The Two Witnesses 57

JESUS Is Now The King Of The Jews 62

The Seventh And Last Trumpet Is Blown 63

The Solid Power Of Heaven and The Lamb Show

Victory 82

The Last Harvest Of Souls From The Earth 87

God's Final Wrath Here On Earth 90

The Final Destruction Of Babylon Begins 99

Babylon The Great Prostitute 105

Satan Is Bound For 1,000 Years...................... 126

Satan Is Released For A Short Time 128

The Great White Throne Judgment Of God.................131

The Alpha & Omega, The Beginning & The End 135

The New Jerusalem And Its New World 137

Jesus Concludes His Revelation & Invitation To

Mankind.. 140

The Angel Validates The Truth Of Jesus' Revelation 141

Your Own Personal Invitation From Jesus 145

A Warning To The Reader Of Revelation.......................147

Preface

I would never have imagined writing a book about Revelation. There are so many already written, and it is extremely controversial, that I had no desire to tackle another one! I am already a successful writer, but Revelation was last on my list for another book to write! God kept prompting me, I kept saying, "that's ridiculous!", and He kept prompting me anyway! Well, that is the way God is when He wants you do something. I finally gave in and began the ride of my life! I would say, if you think you know all about something, think twice if God is trying to tell you something. I learned incredible things!

God showed me a profound simplicity to this very unique book from Jesus Christ Himself. He showed me that Jesus has come one last time to make sure we know who He is, that He loves us at all costs, and wants us with Him forever; like it should be. He showed me that the most important message in the whole book is Jesus' love for His creation.

The next biggest message is that your greatest enemy, Satan, is definitely going down forever. Jesus does not want anyone following him to his horrible abode.

When I realized how important the message is, I became a willing author. I used the Amplified Bible for the scripture quotes. The Amplified Bible gives added meaning to the English translation, since our English words don't always depict the full meaning of the Greek and Hebrew original words. Most languages have a larger concept built right into the word used but our English language doesn't always do that. The Living Bible does a similar thing as a paraphrase.

I also felt like this particular book needed pictures to help make it "real". Unfortunately, we had to use black and white pictures so you wouldn't have to pay so much for your book! I want to recognize my artist the Lord gave me to help with this:

This wonderful and unique artist is Robert Fletcher. He has put his heart and soul into the pictures he has provided. He is a prime example of what God can do in your life, as well. He serves Jesus Christ with vim, vigor and vitality! He has been through the hard times just like the rest of us. I thank God for him.

My prayer is that everyone who reads this book will be blessed and have a much clearer picture of the profound, but simple, message from Jesus, Himself. My goal is to help more of you accept Jesus' invitation and live with Him forever.

Apostle John on the island of Patmos

Introduction

The book of Revelation is the very last book in the Bible. It has been the subject of controversies and diverse interpretations. A good portion of the book of Revelation appears to be symbolic of things to come, making it a challenge to understand. As a result, a great many people just avoid it.

One thing that we do need to understand is that this book is meant to give everyone a profound message that we **must** understand if we want to live with Jesus forever and take as many people with us as possible! Jesus has not put it there to confuse or confound us, rather that Jesus, Himself, has come to all His creation one last time to make it known to the whole world how vitally important the "end of the story" really is! His sole purpose in giving His life for us was to open the door to final and everlasting victory in reclaiming His very own creation, mankind. It's HIS "baby"! It's His victory!! It is OUR victory if we are His followers!!

The last, and triumphant, book of the Bible is called, "The Revelation Of Jesus Christ". Take time to carefully read the first chapter and let it really soak into your brain, your understanding. This is, indeed, Jesus Christ's **personal** last call to His creation, mankind. He is pleading for each and every one to pay attention before it is too late. Jesus picked His beloved friend, John, to show him incredible things, and ask him to write down in a book what he sees and hears, with the purpose of revealing His heart for restoration and salvation. Jesus also wants everyone to know the final end of all evil in our world.

Jesus, Himself, narrates and directs this production, as it must be accurate, convincing and it must reveal everything we need to know to make good decisions so that we can win in the end. It tears His heart out to think of anyone being outside His kingdom forever. He reveals the best and the worst of it in these last few moments of time as we know it. After all, He lowered Himself to leave His beautiful home to come here and live like one of us, and die the cruelest of deaths, then being miraculously raised back to life again; forever breaking the bonds of sin and death in triumph over OUR fate! Now we have a choice! Now it is up to us to CHOOSE to live in His world; it is a "forever" choice, people!

It may surprise you that the book of Revelation was never meant to be complicated and hard to understand. It was designed to show you three important things:

1. The true power and glory of God
2. The demise of all evil
3. The heart of Jesus for reconciliation with His creation

The theme and message of this book is very plain and simple: Avoid the pitfalls and keep your eyes on Him as He, personally, leads you and guides you to the safety and luxury of the New Jerusalem. Everything else in Revelation is just a component part of the progression of the demise of evil along with Satan's kingdom, and the final triumph of Jesus Christ. Jesus wants us to know that the **door is still open** for everyone to change sides and follow Him into glory. He wants us to know that, at any point in the story, a lost person can renounce the world's evil ways and come out of Satan's kingdom and follow Jesus Christ right on in to His own forever kingdom.

Jesus has revealed the horrors of Satan's worldly kingdom that the masses are part of, and revealed how it will be thoroughly and completely taken down, piece by piece until all that is left is smoking embers. Jesus has also revealed HOW to avoid being part of the ruin. He hopes you will love what He has waiting for you. Most of all, He hopes you will come to understand how very much He loves YOU.

Jesus does not care whether or not you understand all the symbolism; the symbolism is there so that Jesus can find something we are familiar with that will help us get the picture of something we have never seen; occurrences in a dimension we are not in yet. The Bible tells us that we have never seen anything like what Jesus has waiting for us! The mystery and glory of the Father of the universe is about to become clear. The gap between God and His creation is about to come together, and Satan is about to be taken out of the way; He wants you to know that! His huge desire is for you to make the right choice, the choice between going down in smoke and ashes with Satan, or being protected from calamity and joining the wedding supper of the Lamb in heaven, and living in the New Jerusalem forever. That is what this whole story is all about.

Get ready for the "ride" of your life! The final battle to eliminate evil is about to begin. YOU will determine your place in the story. There will be no excuse for ignorance, for now we the have "the rest of the story"; we've read the very last page of history. **We know what to do.**

"Behold, I stand at the door and knock; if anyone hears and listens to and heeds My voice and open the door, I will come in to him." Revelation 3:20.

Our World As It Was And Is

In the beginning God created our whole universe and everything in it. He created all live beings that live in our world. He created the most beautiful place for them all to live. The only rule He made was violated and the result was the beginning of the end of all creation, including mankind. Our world began to decline, began to be less perfect, began to cause pain and death.

As a result of mankind's loss of perfection, the only salvation to be had was a long road to a point in time where God provided a perfect sacrifice for all the imperfection that had entered our world. This perfect sacrifice came to us as God in the flesh. The hope of repair of the damage came through Jesus Christ, our substitute, when He was rejected and crucified, becoming the ONLY One to overcome death and the grave. He came to pave the way back to Jehovah God, Himself, so that we have a real chance to get back to the perfection God meant for us to have in the first place!

Jesus Christ has been here, taught us, offered the last sacrifice for sins, came back to life, triumphed over sin and death, and is in heaven preparing to bring us back into His world of perfection. He is actively finishing what He started. **He wants to make sure for sure we can see the path, be guided by His marvelous Light, and end up where we belong – with Him!!**

Now history has brought us this far, many prophetic events have already taken place, and more prophetic events continue to reveal themselves. Jesus Christ, Himself, enters the picture one last time to make sure we've "got it". He desires us SO extremely that He wants to jump in here and make sure we "hear" Him, make sure we know what's happening, make sure we keep our eyes on Him, make sure we know "the end of the story". Jesus' "last ditch effort" to reach us is this book of Revelation, given personally from Him in great detail, to the apostle John so we can know exactly what He is doing to take down ALL evil and bring us back into His perfect world. This is the one and only reason He was willing to go through the agony of the cross, to make it all possible.

A Bit Of History

As Jesus went about His ministry, choosing His apostles and teaching all who would listen, His best friend was John the apostle. From time to time, the gospels mention John as being close to Jesus. It is no surprise that John was the last living apostle that had actually walked and ministered with Jesus, and had been the only apostle spared from a cruel death. Instead, he was banished to the prison island of Patmos for preaching the gospel of Christ. It was no accident that John had been spared for the last visitation from Christ, personally, to allow John to relay this all-important LAST CALL for salvation before the end of time, when it will be too late for His creation to ever have another chance to be redeemed.

So, the story of Jesus Christ's last call to us unfolds. The apostle John is now a very old man who has been banished for life to the small and harsh island of Patmos. By this time, the original church in Jerusalem had been gloriously established on the day of Pentecost and led by the Holy Spirit through the apostles, becoming the example for Christ's church in our world, for our world. The church in Jerusalem became the springboard for spreading the gospel story of salvation to both the Jews and the gentiles, alike, in all the world.

This original church was the checkpoint for establishing churches everywhere else. All missions went out from Jerusalem, all questions were answered there by the very men, the apostles, that Jesus personally taught and the Holy Spirit had personally implemented. Together, the Holy Spirit led them into ALL truth, as He does for us today. Jesus told His apostles that the Comforter, the Holy Spirit, would come in His place to be continually with each one of His believers, making sure we understand the truth.

The apostle Paul was chosen by Jesus Christ, personally, after the Jerusalem church was established. Paul calls himself "an apostle out of season", because he had missed Christ's life, crucifixion and resurrection, as well as the introduction of the church on Pentecost. Paul was an established scholar in the Jewish community, well respected and eager to annihilate anything that was different. He was about the most pure, perfect and powerful Jewish man around! Would you believe **that** is why Jesus chose him? Jesus chose him to lay the foundation in the whole world for every true church that has come into existence in the Gentile world!

Paul attached himself to the church in Jerusalem for his mission trips, and checked in there as his home base for Truth. Paul was the very one who established the seven churches of Asia mentioned here in Revelation. When Jesus picked Paul as an apostle, He knew He would be using these very churches as an example for US today in His Revelation!

Paul was such a very special, chosen person for ministry that, after a while, Jesus took Paul into the "third heaven", much like John, to see for himself the spectacular wonders and majesty of His world. Paul saw such wonders that he couldn't even begin to describe them to us. He truly saw our future world and witnessed the very things Jesus said, "Eye hath not seen or ear heard the things that God is preparing for our eternal existence"!! It was so spectacular, it was beyond anything Paul could describe in human language! Wow! What a God we belong to!

The apostle John had been an eye witness of everything that had taken place, from Jesus' ministry, crucifixion, death, resurrection and ascension back to heaven; as well as the beginning of the church on Pentecost, all of the apostle Paul's missionary journeys and subsequent beheading in Rome. He had been a witness to all the good and all the bad that had taken place to give us the final phase of God's Plan for our eternal salvation. John was well qualified to receive and record this last salvation call from Jesus Christ, Himself.

With the church well-established and spreading rapidly throughout the known world, John was the last of the original witnesses of it all. He was most likely the only one who had seen it all. It is no wonder that Jesus chose him to accurately record His personal message to all of mankind as He makes His LAST CALL to all who will listen. In this last book of God's Word to us He wants to make sure we know Jesus Christ's final message to all of mankind. John will be able to say, like the apostle Paul,

"I have fought a good fight, I have firmly kept the faith, I have finished the race, therefore is laid up for me the victor's crown of righteousness – for being right with God and doing right – which the Lord, the righteous judge, will award me and recompense me on that day…" II Timothy 4:7, 8

Jesus Comes To John With His Final Message

As the book of Revelation begins, it is identified as the revelation of Jesus Christ, Himself, with the help of God's angel, for all of creation to read. Right here in the very beginning of Revelation Jesus makes sure we know who He is and why it is so important to Him that we know how much He cares for us.

"This is the revelation of Jesus Christ. God gave it to Him to disclose and make known to His bond servants certain things that must shortly come to pass in their entirety. And He sent and communicated it with His angel messenger to His bond servant John, who has testified and vouched for all that he saw [in his visions], the Word of God and the testimony of Jesus Christ... May grace be granted to you and spiritual peace from Him Who is and Who was and Who is to come, and from the seven-fold Holy Spirit before His throne. And from Jesus Christ the faithful and trustworthy Witness, the Firstborn of the dead, and the

Prince of the kings of the earth. To Him Who ever loves us, Who has once [for all] loosed and freed us from our sins by His own blood, and formed us into a kingdom, priests to His God and Father – to Him be the glory and the power and the majesty and the dominion throughout the ages and forever and ever. Amen,

Behold He comes with the clouds and every eye shall see Him...'I am the Alpha and the Omega, the Beginning and the End ', says the Lord God, He Who is and Who was and Who is to come, the Almighty (the Ruler of all)." Revelation 1:1-8

John identifies himself as a Christian and fellow partner in Christ, isolated to live on Patmos because of preaching the gospel. As he was worshipping, he heard a voice behind him saying,

"I am the Alpha, the First and the Last. Write promptly what you see in a book and send it to the seven churched which are in Asia..."

When John turned around, he saw Jesus, Himself, standing there in all His glory! John fell at His feet in awe, and Jesus laid His hand on John, telling him not to be afraid. Again, Jesus said to him,

"I am the First and the Last, and the Everlasting One…I died, but see, I am alive for evermore, and I possess the keys of death and Hades (the realm of the dead). Write, therefore, the things you see, what they signify what is to take place hereafter…" *Revelation 1:17-19*

This last message from Jesus, Himself, is very **plain and simple**. His message to us all basically has only three parts that all point to the eternal salvation He offers. Jesus' spoken intent for this special book is to give us all a major look at how God is going to take down Satan's kingdom here on earth, and show us all the glorious things He will do for our eternal well-being. In spite of all the confusion and multiple opinions of what all the symbolism means, the intended message remains simple and direct. John writes:

"I was in the Spirit on the Lord's day, and I heard behind me a great voice like the calling of a war trumpet, saying, 'I am the Alpha and the Omega, the First and the Last. Write promptly

what you see (your vision) in a book and send it to the seven churches which are in Asia...'" Rev. 1:10,11

So, on this most historical day, John begins an amazing and breath-taking journey with Jesus, as He leads John through the warnings to the churches (His kingdom and bride), and on through the progression of Jesus' complete takedown and annihilation of Satan's evil kingdom in our world, and the glorious and spectacular eternal home for those who believe in Him.

Jesus' Message To The Seven Churches

At this time, the original church in Jerusalem had been established through the promised Holy Spirit's guidance, and had spread throughout the known world. Those churches had been established and mentored by the apostles themselves, along with those who had been personally mentored by them. At this time, these churches were alive, each functioning as a community of believers. Jesus chose seven of these churches, who represented different regions, to use as examples to show us how to please God in **our** churches. Jesus is very clear and direct as He urges us to pay close attention to the principle things we must do please God and stay out of Satan's worldly kingdom that is about to be demolished.

It is very important for us to pay attention and take a good look at the things these churches were doing right and what they were doing wrong. Jesus singles out each of the seven churches one at a time, but we can look at all seven on a "do's and don'ts" list. You will notice that Jesus didn't ask them to do the impossible, but rather to get back to how they had been taught in the beginning. So, here is what the Spirit is saying to the churches:

Doing Right	**Doing Wrong**
• Keeping God's Word	• Spiritually dead
• Patient endurance	• Lack of good works for Christ
• Intolerance of wickedness	• False leadership
• Spiritually rich	• Lost enthusiasm for the Lord
• Suffering willingly for Christ	• Believe in Balaam *Rev. 2:14*
• Love, faith and service	• Sexual vice
• Numerous works for the Gospel	• False prophets & prophetesses
• Enthusiastic belief	• Too comfortable
	• Faith in riches

These are the rewards and results of our actions:

Rewards	**Rewards**
• Eat from the Tree of Life	• Remove your place in God's kingdom
• Receive the Crown of Life	

- Eat hidden manna
- Have a new name
- Authority and power over nations
- Robes of white
- Jesus will speak in your behalf
- Keep you from the hour of trial
- Become a pillar in God's synagogue
- Sit beside Jesus on His throne
- Dine with Jesus

- Pressing distress & anguish
- All kinds of afflictions
- Death – separation from God
- Will go through the hour of trial. *Rev.3:10*

The churches were (and still are!) much like a young couple who get married, get on with their exciting life, get in a routine, getting very familiar and used to each other and losing some of the initial enthusiasm they started out with. The Great Commission was given to all believers by Jesus, Himself, as the number one focus of our lives in His kingdom; spreading the gospel story to everyone in the world. The Great Commission is not just something we **practice**, but it is a **way of life 24/7.** As believers, we are to **never** stop representing Jesus Christ and His gospel as long as we live on this earth.

We don't just have the gospel, we ARE the gospel! When we ARE the gospel, we are "practicing what we preach"! The world will never listen to you unless you ARE the real thing, being like Christ.

When we keep our focus and our enthusiasm we attract those that need Christ in their lives. The believers who were still practicing the Great Commission were the very ones who were still in God's good graces here in John's record. Those who had gotten lazy, who had diverted their attention to other things, who had allowed wickedness to creep in to the church, etc., were the ones about to lose their position in God's kingdom. Much like the bride and groom, the "new" had worn off and they had gotten "ho-hum" about living for Jesus. Here in His "last call", Jesus is gracious enough to show them what they must do before it is too late. As believers, ourselves, this part of the Revelation story is most certainly for US today. Thank God for giving us a chance to look at this as a **wakeup call** so we, ourselves, have a chance to correct our own condition! **That is what this part is for!** Jesus is adamant about us getting it right and helping others to get it right.

The Great Commission means joining Him in reaching out to others any way we can with His "last call". **This the last call of the Great Commission;** this the last call for all of eternity that anyone will ever have, to live in the perfect world of Jesus Christ.

Jesus' Invitation Continues

Jesus, once again, says,

"Behold I stand at the door and knock, if anyone hears and listens to and heeds My voice and opens the door, I will come in to him and will eat with him and he with Me. He who overcomes (is victorious), I will grant to him to sit beside Me on My throne, as I Myself overcame (was victorious) and sat down beside My Father on His throne." Rev.3:20,21

As Jesus is pleading with us to "open the door" and let Him into our lives, He shows us that **heaven, itself, has its door open for us** to behold what is happening on our behalf. The Holy Spirit gives John the privilege of being there to observe all these activities in the spirit realm:

"I looked, and lo, a door standing open in heaven!...lo, a throne stood in heaven, with One seated on the throne!" Rev. 4:1

This scene is the wide open invitation from all of heaven, looking down on God's created world in anticipation of God's last call to mankind to repent of their sins and be saved from the destruction that is eminent. The wide open door continues, showing all of creation the glory of their Savior, with all the angels and people who have already been redeemed in heaven with Him; every elder and creature in heaven worshipping the Savior of the world. Wow!! What a spectacular sight! Makes you want to be there!

Jesus wants to personally show us heaven's wide-open door and all the glory of heaven so we will make a decision to be there! You will see, as the Revelation story unfolds, that Jesus is right there all the time earnestly hoping that more unsaved people will open their hearts and come out of the destruction of Satan's kingdom while they can. You will see that He even makes a comment in several places, in between all the horror of it, all the way through the take-down of Satan's network of evil, before heaven's wide-open door closes forever to mankind's salvation.

Preparation Begins For
The Final Victory

Satan has ruled our world ever since Adam and Eve decided to sin in the Garden of Eden. Sin meant death for them at some point in their lives. At that time in history there was NO salvation available to them; if they had gone ahead and eaten from the Tree of Life in their sinful condition, they would have been lost forever, separated from their Creator. God did not create mankind just to turn around and allow them to be destroyed and separated from Him. Sadly, He had no choice other than to banish them from Eden to keep them from being lost forever, until He could bring in a way of redemption for all of mankind.

The Beginning Of The End

If Adam and Eve had eaten from the Tree Of Life in their sinful state, they would have sealed their fate for sure, by being permanently sealed in their sin, and so would we. God did not create us for destruction, but for life with Him!

Jesus Christ was already willing to take on their sin to Himself and die on the cross, bury their sin, and redeem them for eternity. God had banished them from Eden to save their eternal lives! God even placed angels, with fiery swords, at the only gate to Eden, to prevent Adam and Eve from returning, with possibility of being eternally doomed. Jesus actually saved them from permanent death (separation from Him) at the very beginning of time! Now, here in Revelation, He is guiding John in writing down a final message in a book for all of mankind! Jesus Christ is **determined** to get you back, to get back every single person that is willing to repent of his/her sins and follow Him into His eternity! His heart is turned inside out, earnestly urging YOU and ME to be on His side.

This is his last chance to save us, OUR last chance to accept His offer.

As the "story of the end" of all things begins, Jesus has made sure we know WHO He is and WHAT this book is all about. He has shown us the examples of what His followers are doing right and what they are doing wrong, along with the consequences of both. Now He is ready to take a deep breath and show YOU and ME exactly how Satan's kingdom is coming down, as well as how Jesus Christ's true kingdom will come about for all of eternity.

As we look through John's eyes into the **open** heavens, lo and behold, there is a spectacular, breath-taking view of a throne with fiery gemstones, flashes of lightening and peals of thunder, a bright rainbow encircling the throne. A glassy sea seems to emit from the throne, along with fiery torches that represent the seven Spirits of God. There are four super intelligent creatures guarding the throne, and 24 elders, who are the heavenly Sanhedrin, falling prostrate, throwing down their crowns and declaring glory and honor to Him Who created all things, being worthy to receive all glory and honor.

The One seated on the throne in heaven had a scroll in His open hand. The scroll had writing on the front and back and was sealed with seven seals. A strong angel appeared announcing in a loud voice, *"Who is worthy to open the scroll and to break the seals?"* Sadly enough, there was no one in heaven or on the earth that could open any of it! John began to weep out loud, very bitterly. Suddenly, one of the elders told John to stop crying and pay attention to the Lion of Judah, the Root of David, Who had won the right to open the scroll!

As John looked up, he saw a Lamb standing in front of the throne, appearing on the throne. The four living creatures and the 24 elders began to worship Him, holding the **golden bowls of the believer's prayers** while singing a new song.

As the Lamb (Jesus) opens the seals of the scroll, each episode is represented by a horse. Each time a seal is opened, an elder, a living creature or an angel bids John to come and see what it is. All seven seals must be opened and accomplished before Satan's kingdom of evil can be taken down. **Heaven's doors are still open and Jesus is still calling for more people to repent and be saved before it is too late.**

All of heaven is cheering in anticipation of the Lamb opening the seals of the scroll:

You are worthy to take the scroll and to break the seals that are on it, for You were slain (sacrificed) and with Your blood You purchased men unto God from every tribe and language and people and nation. And You have made them a kingdom (royal race) and priests to our God, and they shall reign over the earth!" *Rev. 5:9, 10*

As they sang to the Lamb, ten thousand of ten thousands, thousands of angels joined them singing loudly:

"Deserving is the Lamb, Who was sacrificed, to receive all the power and riches and wisdom and might and honor and majesty (glory and splendor) and blessing!" Rev. 5:11,12

As they sang, every created thing in heaven and on earth and under the earth (in Hades, the place of the departed dead spirits), and on the sea and all that are in it, joined them in the loud songs and praises to God and the Lamb!

Can you imagine how much John was overwhelmed with awe at this breath-taking sight?? As he looked, he saw the Lamb begin to open the seals of the scroll. Because we cannot possibly comprehend all that God is doing, Jesus and John use representations familiar to us to show us what is taking place. Jesus, Himself, initiates the process. These are the things that He must do to help finalize these events of the end of Satan's worldly network.

As John and all of heaven watch in anticipation, the seven seals of the scroll are opened and the earth begins to experience the beginning of the end of Satan's kingdom network, with all of mankind who are participating in it and refusing to come out from it.

Up until now, Satan has managed to build his network of deceit and lies in a venue of apparent attractiveness, affecting all aspect of human life here on earth. Commerce and daily life have become built on Satan's foundation of smoothed-over lies and corruption in leadership and commerce. He has done such a superb job of hoodwinking the public that the whole world, in general, has bought in to it. This is the very urgent reason Jesus, Himself, is here with John opening the very doors of heaven to reveal His all-out last invitation to come out of Satan's kingdom and live with Him in His eternal world!

Several things have to happen before it will do any good to take down Satan's network of evil and reclaim mankind. The very first thing Jesus must do is to remove the blinders that prevent people from seeing their own condition as it really is, to help them open their eyes to the reality of where they have allowed themselves to be. Of course Jesus has been urging them, through His believers, to see the reality of sin and its consequences, but as Solomon said in Proverbs, the "madding crowd" just keeps on going right on down the wide, but wrong, avenue without a second thought. Solomon says "Wisdom" cries out to these people and they are oblivious, paying no attention. Now Jesus is ready to literally stand in front of this oblivious crowd, waving His arms and saying, "come out while you still can!" This is the last call; read my lips!

For the first time in the history of mankind, it has come time for God to reckon with Satan over His creation that has been ruined by the rascal. In the very beginning, God Eve that Satan would bruise the heel of her offspring, but her offspring would in turn bruise Satan's head. Satan has been biting at mankind's heel for all of time up to this point. He can only bite the heel, not the head! Now it is time for Eve's offspring to bite Satan's head! That means a death blow, that means he is presently going down, losing the battle for the souls of mankind. Hallelujah!!!

Now, Jesus has been chosen to open the seals of the scroll, allowing the beginning of the **preparation of the earth** for the weakening of Satan's network of evil. The earth needs to see Satan as he really is, allowing evil to culminate into it's end result.

As Jesus opens each seal, He is calling for mankind to wake up and run away from Satan's territory and be saved. As the seven seals of the scroll are opened, each prepares the earth for the next one. The seals are opened:

1. **First seal** – a white horse appears whose rider was carrying a bow, and was given a crown to go out and conquer as much of the world as he could before anything else proceeded to happen.

2. **Second seal** – a flaming red horse appears whose rider had been given a huge sword and the power to **remove peace** from the earth so that mankind slaughtered each other without mercy.

3. **Third seal** – a menacing black horse appears whose rider has a balancing scale in his hands, declaring astronomical prices for necessities except for oil and wine.

4. **Forth seal** – a bruised and battered looking pale horse appeared whose rider's name is Death. Hades (the place of the departed souls) followed closely after him. They were given authority and power over one forth of the earth to kill with the sword, cause famine and plagues and disease, and death by wild animals.

5. **Fifth seal** – a crowd of martyred souls at the foot of God's altar are crying out for justice. They are given beautiful, flowing robes, and told to be patient until the rest of the earth's martyrs have been added to their number.

6. **Sixth seal** – There was a great earthquake; the sun grew black and the full disc of the moon became as blood. The stars dropped to the earth as if they were

shaken by an out-of-season wind. The sky rolled up like a scroll and vanished! Every island and mountain was dislodged from its place.

Then the kings of the earth with all their noblemen, magistrates, military, the wealthy. the strong and everyone (whether slave or free) ran into the mountains to hide among the rocks. As they ran from God's wrath and vengeance, they cried for the rocks to fall on them in its wake. They recognized that God is on His throne, getting ready to pour out His vengeance on to the earth! The great day of God's wrath toward evil has come! **The reality is here!**

There were four angels of destruction stationed at the four corners of the earth, holding back the four winds of the earth and sea, until the **righteous servants of God had been secured by the seal of God.** As John looked on, an angel came flying from the East carrying the **seal of God**, crying out to the four angels holding back the wind, not to harm anything until all of the servants of God have been marked with God's seal on their foreheads.

Twelve thousand people out of each tribe of Israel were chosen, plus a vast number of people no one could count, that had come from every conceivable place on earth. Together, they were all marked with the seal of God to separate them out of Satan's kingdom, because they had all accepted Jesus Christ as their Savior and King. These were all the Christians, both Jews and gentiles.

As John looked on, one of the 24 elders, worshipping around the throne, asked John if he knew who these people were. John said no, so the elder told him they were the righteous people who had been redeemed from the earth and the great tribulation, who had washed their robes in the blood of the Lamb. They are all worshipping God and the Lamb Who shelters them from all evil, wipes away every tear and lets them drink from the streams of living water that flow forever.

Six of the seven seals have been opened by Jesus, and now He is getting ready to open the last seal that opens to a succession of major events in God's preparation to annihilate Satan's kingdom.

The Seventh Seal

Now the Lamb is ready to open the seventh and final seal of God. This seal holds all the rest of the major **events of the preparation** of all of heaven and earth for the final conquering of Satan and his evil network. The opening of this seal is so profound that there is silence in heaven for thirty minutes. This seal reveals a succession of events that have never occurred in all of time here on earth.

All of these events are huge, earth-shaking and powered by God, Himself. Everything that happens from now on will lead to the day Satan's kingdom goes up in smoke; THE final end of ALL the damager he has ever done!! These events of the seventh and last seal will also show you how important your prayers, your faith and your trust in Jesus really are; they are the clockwork of the victory for your soul!

Event #1 Seven angels prepare to blow their trumpets.

As the seventh seal is opened, the same seven angels, of God's preparation, are lined up and poised, standing before Father God, Himself, and each one is given a trumpet to announce more pending disasters for the unrepentant earth. The disasters are designed to wake up the unrepentant world to the **last call of Jesus Christ to repent and be saved.**

Event#2 Prayers of the believers are mixed with God's incense from His altar.

As the seven angels prepare to blow their trumpets, a very important occasion occurs. Another angel appears and hovers over heaven's altar with a golden censor very full of fragrant incense to mingle it with all the **prayers of all God's believers.** The smoke of the incense, mixed with the prayers of God's people, arose in the presence of God.

Don't think for a minute that your prayers go unanswered, don't think for a moment that your prayers are not important to Father God! Every single prayer of His believers is a huge part of everything He is doing to cover you, protect you and bring down the greatest enemy of all time, Satan. God is bringing Satan down because of you, because He wants to redeem you and give the home of all homes, living in His presence for all of eternity. YOU are the reason!! Your prayers are vitally important to Him.

Now that the seven angels have received their trumpets, and the prayers of the believers are mixed with the incense of God, the angel of the heavenly altar filled his censor with fiery coals of incense from the altar. He cast it upon the earth in preparation for the events that are about to happen as each angel blows his trumpet that will release damaging signs to the unbelievers on earth.

Event #3 The first four angels blow their trumpets.

The first angel blows his trumpet. There was a storm of hail and fire mixed with blood cast upon the earth. The result was that one third of trees were burned up along with all the green grass.

The second angel blows his trumpet. John says that something resembling a great mountain was blazing with fire and was hurled into the sea. The sea turned to blood, making the destruction so great that one third of its living creatures died, and one third of the ships on the sea were destroyed.

The third angel blows his trumpet. A huge star fell from heaven, burning like a torch. It's name is "Wormwood". It fell on one third of the rivers and springs of water, and poisoned them so that many people died from using the water.

The fourth angel blows his trumpet. One third of the sun, moon and stars were smitten so that they were darkened, one third of the daylight was withdrawn, as well as one third of the light at night was kept from shining.

As John was observing all this wonder, he saw a solitary eagle flying through the middle of heaven crying with a loud voice, *"Woe, woe, woe to those who dwell on earth, because of the rest of the trumpet blasts which the three angels are about to sound!"* In other words, it is about to get much worse, as God is not done with the earth that has become alien to His plan to redeem mankind.

As the last three angels blow their trumpets, there are three events about to happen that are called **"woes".** These "woes" happen right along with all the **preparation** for the final blow to Satan and his evil kingdom.

Event #4 The fifth angel blows his trumpet, also introducing the first "woe".

John sees a star fall from the sky to the earth, and to the angel was given a key to the shaft of the Abyss (the bottomless pit). The angel took the key and opened the shaft of the Abyss, and massive smoke, like the smoke from a huge furnace, billowed out of the long shaft; so much smoke that it darkened the sun and the whole atmosphere.

Then out of the smoke came locusts on to the earth who were granted the power of terrible scorpions. Their marching orders were to not harm any of the earth's trees and plants, but only to attack such humans that do not have the **mark of God** on their foreheads. You remember that God has held back the progression of His recompense long enough for all the **believers to be marked with His seal** on their foreheads, where the mark would be fully visible. God's distinguishing mark identifies the believers as belonging to Him, coming under His personal protection of them during all the final events of the destruction of Satan's kingdom.

It is very interesting, here, that quite a bit of detail is given to the description of the locusts, their orders and their activities. They actually play a major part in the seriousness and the progression of the weakening and disabling of the power Satan has had throughout time to ruin every aspect of God's creation anywhere he could to spoil the life God intended for mankind. The things that God has to do now, to bring him down, are earth-shaking, almost incomprehensible to us.

The release of the locusts in the smoke of the Abyss is horrifying! They were commanded to severely torment all those who did not have the **seal of God** on their foreheads. They were not permitted to kill the people of the earth, just torment them for five months. The torment was like the continual stinging of a big scorpion.

The locusts resembled horses equipped for battle. Their faces looked like people wearing golden crowns. They had long hair and teeth like a lion. They had scales like a breastplate of iron, and the whirring of their wings was like a vast number of chariots going full speed into battle. Their weapons are their tails that sting like a scorpion to hurt people for five months. Their king??....the angel of the Abyss, none other than Satan, himself! His name is Apollyon (destroyer). Now the real truth is coming out about this cunning deceiver! He's not beautiful anymore; his real face is showing!

Event #5 The sixth angel blows his trumpet, also introduces the second "woe", a taste of Hell.

Now a solitary voice is heard, coming from the altar with four horns that stands before God, speaking to the angel that blew the sixth trumpet, *"Liberate the four angels that are bound at the great river Euphrates…"* Remember that, just after the sixth seal was opened by the Lamb, there were four angels, stationed at the four corners of the earth, who had been given the authority and power to injure the earth and sea, were now holding back the destructive winds while God's angel marked the believers with the seal of God. Those receiving the seal of God were never to be harmed by any of the devastation about to happen.

Now, as part of the events released by the sixth trumpet, it is finally time for the four angels to release their hold on the destructive winds they were assigned to hold back. Now it is time for the winds to destroy one third of unsaved mankind!

Now you think the locusts were horrifying when they were stinging mankind? That was a mild comparison to what comes next! **This is what the four angels released:** 200,000,000 troops on horseback! This is what the troops looked like:

- The riders wore breastplates of fiery red, sapphire blue and sulphur yellow.
- The horses' heads looked like lion's heads, and from their mouths poured out fire, smoke and sulphur (same as brimstone), their tails were like biting snakes.

The **fire, smoke and sulphur** that poured from the horses' mouths were **plagues** that killed one third of unsaved mankind. The fire, smoke and sulphur are a taste of **Hell** itself! The horses' biting tails are just adding more injury like a good swift kick to the rear! The heat and the pressure is on!! Now even these unbelievers have a pretty good idea what Hell is all about!! BUT…

Even after this devastating and horrifying event, these people who are still alive **did not REPENT!!** Even after all that has happened, all the gross horrors, people STILL didn't acknowledge God, believe on Jesus Christ their Savior! This has got to be the epitome of stubbornness!! But, even so, Jesus loves them SO much that He is STILL here holding out in the hope that someone will repent!

You would think, by now, the people who are left alive would be scared to death and begin to understand the power behind the devastation. But people are as stubborn as the day is long, and hold on to their pride. This is what Revelation has to say about their stubbornness and rebellion:

*"And the rest of humanity who were not killed by the plagues even then **did not repent** of [the worship of] the works of their (own) hands, so as to cease paying homage to the demons and*

*idols of silver and gold and bronze and stone and wood, which can neither see, nor hear, nor move. And they **did not repent** of their murders or their practices of magic (sorceries)…"*

When our physical, human body expires, the scriptures teach us that our "forever self" goes back to God Who gave it. The life of all heavenly living beings is also eternal; yes, including Satan. **There is no record, in the scriptures, of God ever making any living being non-existent.** There are some current religions that actively teach that life ceases to exist when we die. The death that we die simply puts us in to another dimension of God's world; only our physical body is dead.

If you remember, God told Adam and Eve they would surely die if they ate of the Tree Of Good And Evil. Satan came along and told them that they wouldn't die. Now, who is right?? Satan knew God was talking about an eternal **separation** from God; he also knew that would not happen instantly, so he took advantage of it, and, wallah!!…they did disappear!! Well, who was right?? Actually, they both were right because there is a human body death, and there is a spiritual body death that is eternal. God is interested in our eternal existence. He has taken every step He can to keep us from being separated from Him forever.

Just so you know, "time" is an earth "thing". It belongs only to the earth. Someone has said that "time" is an encapsulated segment of eternity. Because we have never experienced eternity, it is impossible for us to truly comprehend it. I have heard that the closest thing to understanding it is a **circle** that appears to have no beginning or end. I believe it is vital for us humans to believe we are eternal beings, and we will exist **somewhere** forever. God knows it. That is the very reason He MUST get Satan out of the way and contained. Satan will never die either, but he can be and will be contained, never to have access to any of us ever again, if we choose to believe in Jesus Christ as the Son of God, that paved our way back to Father God!! Hallelujah!

I cannot comprehend anyone being obstinate enough to be willing to take a chance on the **only other option; unbelief**! The other option? Living forever in the torment that was originally meant only for Satan and his fallen angels. I used to have a bumper sticker that said, "God loves you whether you like it or not!". That is exactly how He feels toward all of humanity!! A person can run and jump and play, and follow any rabbit trail he/she wants to follow, live life just for himself/herself, ignoring God all they want to, but it changes nothing in God's righteous plan to save mankind on HIS terms. God WILL march on, He WILL contain Satan, and believers in Jesus WILL live happily ever after!!

Can you believe God's creation, mankind, could be so stubborn and defiant in the face of these horrifying events?? Way back in the Old Testament, King Solomon called these people "the madding crown", who go on their merry, oblivious way to nowhere! Solomon was gifted by God to be the wisest person who ever lived. This is what he says,

"Wisdom cries aloud in the street, she raises her voice in the markets, she cries at the head of the noisy intersections [of the chief gathering places]; at the entrance of the city gates she speaks: 'How long, O simple ones [open to evil], will you love being simple? And the scoffers delight on scoffing and [self-confident] fools hate knowledge? If you will turn and (repent) and give heed to my reproof, behold, I [Wisdom] will pour out My spirit upon you,

I will make known My words known to you…whoso harkens to Me [Wisdom] shall dwell securely and in confident trust and shall be quiet, without fear of dread or evil."' Proverbs 1:20-23

Solomon lived and wrote a long time ago. Unfortunately, people haven't changed! If you are following the crowd, you are certain to end up in the wrong place! While we are hearing from Solomon, let's hear what he has to say about the **outcome** of the ways of those who **refuse** to open their eyes and "smell the coffee".

God has given mankind His affection, as well as His discipline, ever since the Garden of Eden. He has given us a way out of our mess by sacrificing His only Son to take the rap for our mistakes and sins, and give us **perpetual forgiveness.** He did all that to redeem us from evil and to give us a home He has prepared for us! The only thing He has ever asked from us is **repentance** and **belief** in Him. **God never changes.** His plan for us is the same as it was in the days of Solomon.

The book of Revelation is the record of God's plan playing out to its glorious and spectacular end, in triumph over evil.

What you read here in Solomon's writings, of the outcome for stubborn people, is essentially the same as the outcome in Revelation for stubborn and rebellious people that refuse to commit to Father God and Jesus Christ His Son. This is what Proverbs predicts will happen to the "madding crowd", all those who are intentionally oblivious to the Truth and righteousness of Father God:

"Because I have called you and you have refused [to answer], I have stretched out My hand and no man [among you] has headed it, and you treated as nothing all My counsel and would accept none of My reproof, I will also laugh at your calamity; I will mock when the thing comes upon you that shall cause terror and panic — when your panic come with a storm and desolation, and your calamity comes as a whirlwind, when distress and anguish come upon you. **Then** *will they call upon Me [Wisdom] but I will not answer, they will seek Me early and diligently but will not find Me. Because they* **hated knowledge** *and did not* **choose** *the reverent and worshipful fear of the Lord, would accept none of My counsel, and despised all My reproof, therefore,* **shall they eat the fruit of their own way** *and be satiated with their own devices. For the* **backsliding** *of the simple shall* **slay** *them, and*

the **carelessness of self-confident fools shall destroy them.**"
Proverbs 1:24-33

The thing is, God created ALL of us in His own likeness, He gave us living and active parts of Himself, and He gave us the breath of life. He even gave us a GPS, called a conscience, so His Holy Spirit could come and live there to keep us on track; that is, IF we will allow it to be there, not messing up the GPS! When we choose God to direct our lives, He graciously gives us a greater part of His knowledge that only comes when we accept Jesus Christ as our Savior and Advocate. **The knowledge and wisdom that God gives to believers is designed to give them an advantage over the world's knowledge.** *I Corinthians 1:29, 2:10.*

All of mankind has the same offer from God, but the **choice** is ours and ours alone. God will never make that decision FOR us; we, ourselves, will take the consequences of our very own decisions. It is solely up to each person to **choose** their own destination. There will be road signs all along the way, but the arrival at our destination is clearly up to our own choice.

God, Himself, has prepared the earth for this very moment in time. Jesus Christ has come in person to plead with His precious creation to come out of Satan's kingdom and be with Him instead. Jesus has taken every opportunity to offer salvation to everyone left on the earth. He does not want anyone to go down with the false kingdom of Satan. **Everything possible has been done to save mankind from an eternity of torture and separation from God.** Now it is time to eliminate everything Satan has created on the earth that harms mankind. The very conflagration of Hell, itself, will permanently destroy it all.

Satan's influence upon mankind will be no more. He is a "stand alone" renegade about to be chained and cast into the bottomless pit, the Abyss. He will never again be able to build a kingdom for himself. **He is finished forever.**

Event #6

As the events of the sixth seal continue to unfold, John sees another mighty angel coming down from heaven, robed in a cloud with a rainbow over his head, his face is like the sun, and his feet and legs are like columns of fire. If you remember, God's protection is represented, in the Bible, as a **cloud** of protection by day, and a pillar of **fire** by night, in the book of Exodus as the Israelites crossed the desert on their way back to their homeland. In the Bible story of Noah, God gave him the sign of the rainbow to represent God's promise to never again flood the whole earth. The sun always represents light versus darkness. Many times the Bible makes it clear that Jesus is the "Light of the world", and clears away all darkness.

As this angel comes down from heaven, he is representing ALL of God's **promises** of wisdom, knowledge, protection and triumph over darkness. He is holding a small scroll as he places his right foot on the sea and his left foot on the land. He shouts with a loud voice, like the roar of a lion, and seven thunders responded with a distinct message. As John was about to record what they said, the angel commanded him to seal it up until further notice, and not write it down! These will be revealed later on.

The same angel raised his right hand toward heaven and swore by the name of Him Who lives forever, Who created all of heaven and earth, that there will be no more waiting or delay, **no more time shall pass until the seventh angel blows the final trumpet blast to announce the completion of all of God's promises to us here on the earth, and the final blow to Satan and his kingdom.** When it comes time for the seventh angel to blow his trumpet, he will be announcing God's mystery, His secret design and hidden purpose will be openly **fulfilled, accomplished and completed.**

To John's surprise, the solitary voice from the heavenly altar, spoke once again directly to John, asking him to take the small scroll, so he asked for it. As the angel handed it to him, he instructed to eat the scroll, and that it would taste sweet in his mouth, but would give him a sour stomach! How unusual!! He actually ate the scroll! Can you imagine?? You remember John had been caught up into the heavenly realm to witness all the events he is supposed to record in a book, which means that John is currently in a spiritual time-warp, so to speak, when he is instructed to eat the scroll. John ate the scroll and experienced just what the angel had said. It was sweet as honey in his mouth, but by the time it settled in his stomach, it made his stomach sour.

The meaning of this episode is this: The events, that John is about to observe and record, are going to be bittersweet, meaning that the victory over Satan and his kingdom will be a sweet relief, but the bitter part is the loss of the precious souls that refuse to repent and follow Jesus.

Event #7 A Great Celebration In Heaven

Can you imagine an earth without all the bad business practices we now have? Can you imagine a world without Satan's kingdom? Wouldn't you think the people that are still on earth at this time would be so terrified they would be willing to repent and follow Jesus! Looking back over all the events before this, the plagues, the destruction, the unprecedented storms all preparing the earth for this moment in time, you would think people would think twice about accepting Jesus' invitation to come away from the world's ways and be saved. Instead, they curse and blaspheme God while they keep right on living their wicked lives, even in their disaster!

In the meantime, heaven is celebrating the demolition of Satan's kingdom, and preparing for the triumphant marriage supper of the Lamb. It starts with a mighty shout from a great crowd in heaven, glorifying and worshipping the Lord God, exclaiming:

"Hallelujah (praise the Lord)! Salvation and glory (splendor and majesty) and power (dominion and authority) to our God! Because His judgments (His condemnation and punishment, His sentences of doom) are true and sound and just and upright). He has judged the great and notorious Harlot, who demoralized and poisoned the earth with her lewdness and adultery (idolatry). And He has avenged the blood of His servants at her hand." Rev. 19:1,2

The celebration and praise to God goes on and on as the smoke of the destruction of Satan's whole evil kingdom ascends into oblivion. **The deed is done!!** God's careful preparation has paid off. **Never** again will Satan be able to rule mankind in this world! He has been left with no one to rule, no one to corrupt and destroy!

Event #8 The Marriage Supper Of The Lamb

As the celebration in heaven continues, the scene turns to the marriage supper of the Lamb. John hears a vast throng shouting like the boom of huge pounding waves and the roar of terrific and mighty peals of thunder, exclaiming:

"Hallelujah! For now the Lord our God the Omnipotent (the all-ruler) reigns! Let us rejoice and shout for joy! Let's celebrate and ascribe Him honor and glory, for the marriage supper of the Lamb has come, and His Bride has prepared herself."

In the New Testament, the church is the Bride of Christ (Ephesians 5, etc). Each believer in Jesus Christ has become a "new creature", allowing God to order and arrange his/her life, changing to God's ways of thinking and doing. **The life a believer lives is his/her preparation for participating in the marriage supper of the Lamb.** Revelation 19:8 reveals the preparation of His Bride,

…His Bride has prepared herself. She has been permitted to dress in fine (radiant) linen, dazzling and white – for the fine linen is (significant and represents) the righteousness (the upright, just and godly living, deeds, and conduct, and right standing with God) of the saints (God's people)."

This bittersweet event that is about to happen is, in fact, what we all wonder about and even dread; that is, being with Jesus in eternity without loved one who refused to repent and follow Jesus. This is a huge concern for most Christians. This bittersweet event is the biggest "tough love" event that has ever occurred! It is based on God's foundational principle of the **free choice** He has allowed all of mankind, even if he/she makes a final bad choice of where to spend eternity.

Even though God's love for ALL will never end, a chance for a relationship with God WILL end if we are stubborn enough to refuse His offer of salvation. When John "ate" the little scroll, he was able to experience the sweetness of God's perfect love for all of humanity, as well as the bitterness of losing those that stubbornly refuse His glorious redemption of mankind.

More than likely, we put our own selves in John's place to feel the bittersweet feeling of our concern for our soul mate, our sons and daughters, our friends and, ultimately, the whole world of people who refuse to surrender to Jesus Christ Who is bringing salvation to anyone who will accept it. He is the only one Who can relieve our tensions and worries now, and guarantee our safe trip to heaven!

At this place in time, our earnest prayers can still go up to heaven and be part of the incense burning on the altar of God, the incense full of the prayers of God's people scattered around the world, to redeem those who are willing to leave Satan's attractive, but evil, kingdom while there is still time. As believers our prayers are powerful mixed with God's own incense and being scattered right here on earth, making His offer to mankind a "sweet offer" for the last and final time.

Event #9 The Two Witnesses

As the events of the sixth trumpet come to a close, **the last event of the sixth trumpet occurs right in the holy city of Jerusalem.** The Jewish people have always been God's chosen nation through which He brought His Son, Jesus Christ, into the world to live an exemplary life, teach the Truth, die and rise again to free the whole world from eminent judgment; the only way out of Satan's evil kingdom here on earth. Time after time, all through history, the Jewish nation has rebelled, worshipped pagan idols, abused God's kindness resulting in their punishment by God by being taking away their privileges and sending them into captivity, time after time.

The two most famous of these captivities were the Egyptian and Babylonian captivities. To make a long story short, they never learned their lesson. Even when Jesus came to our earth, the Romans were occupying their homeland. The Jewish nation was under occupation once again, and, once again, they were still looking for a king to come and save them.

Because the Jewish history of their kings was rich and glorious, they were focusing on a repeat of the pompous, rich and glorious kingdoms like Solomon and David had. The Jewish people were definitely NOT looking for a king that was born in a stable to common parents! They were curious but NOT accepting a savior who wore common clothes, had no identifiable home and walked all over the countryside fraternizing with tax collectors, harlots and fishermen!

Not only did His profile not fit their agenda, Jesus openly chided the leadership of Israel, calling them "whitewashed sepulchers full of dead men's bones"! Jesus meant that they looked good and smelled good on the outside but were rotten on the inside, with bad attitudes and pompous opinions of themselves. He also overturned the tables of the money changers at the temple, saying that they were making a business and market out of God's house of prayer. The Jewish leaders were infuriated by Him.

Ultimately, the Jewish nation actually took it upon themselves the responsibility of crucifying Jesus Christ; they angrily cried out to Pontius Pilate for the blood of Jesus to be on their own heads, when Pilate washed his hands of the responsibility. Even though the massively thick curtain in their temple ripped from top to bottom when Jesus died, even though the sky darkened and an earthquake occurred, even though dead saints got up and walked around the city, the Jewish leaders set their jaws on it being a hoax. They were determined that the Jewish common people would believe it was all a hoax, that Jesus' body was stolen and He never rose from the dead' covering up the resurrection of Jesus Christ the Son of God!

God chose the Jewish nation, with their lineage, to bring Jesus Christ into the world, and creating a written legacy of His time here on earth where He accomplished Hus victory over the doom and loss the world was under because of sin. **All the instructions we need are included on God's written legacy, the Bible.** The Jewish nation has not been successful in discrediting it.

In spite of the Jewish leaders' efforts to keep the status quo and do away with Jesus, the original true believers were Jewish! The original church, established after its birth on the day of Pentecost, was Jewish! Our own Christian origin is Jewish! But sadly enough, the stubbornness and rebellion of the Jews, as a nation, goes on to this present day. The majority of the Jewish people do not accept Jesus Christ as the Son of God, or His crucifixion and resurrection for the purpose of forgiveness of sins. Yes, they are stuck in a time-warp!

As a result of their on-going disbelief in Jesus Christ as their Savior, they have continued to be persecuted, not only in their own land, but wherever they choose to live in the world. They have been scattered among the nations, receiving all kinds of mistreatment from other nations. **BUT**, they have always been, and still are, God's holy nation. God has promised them that He will **gather them back from all nations, and bring them back to their beloved country, as well as their position in God's kingdom.** It is pretty obvious that this has happened in our day and time. Most nations wonder how a little tiny country like Israel can continue to exist in the face of fierce opposition!! Miracle after miracle **keeps** them there!

The fantastic thing that God has promised them is that He will **"open their eyes" to see and feel the magnitude of what they did with Jesus, and they will be filled with remorse and repent as a nation!!**

Here, in the very last event of the sixth trumpet, God is specifically preparing the Jewish people for what they are about to receive and accept; **the true Gospel of Jesus Christ!** The Jews are about to experience the last of their rejections by others, the profoundness of Jehovah God, and the real, earth-shaking truth about Jesus Christ! **They are about to be back in God's good graces for the first time in centuries.** So, Jesus has John introduce the amazing account of the two witnesses; this will be the second **woe.**

The Two Witnesses

As Father God continues His preparations for the final victory over Satan and his massive, tainted and evil kingdom, He sends **His two witnesses** right into the middle of an occupied and trampled-on Jerusalem; which, by the way, is STILL His holy city! Father God is about to **reclaim the city** while He opens the eyes of the Jewish nation to the profoundness of what they did to His Son Jesus, as well as their refusal, all these centuries, to repent and accept Jesus Christ as their true King and Savior. The Jewish nation is about to finally realize what they did, and repent in anguish and tears! **Father God is about to FULFILL His promise to them!!**

The two powerful Witnesses have actually come from heaven. John was told that these two Witnesses were the two olive branches and the two lamp stands that stand before the Lord of the earth. These two Witnesses are representing God's PEACE (as the olive branches), and God's LIGHT (the lamp stands) that He is about to bring to His holy city,

Jerusalem. Once more, the people have a chance to either JOIN or OPPOSE God! **Once again, the Gospel of Jesus Christ is prophesied; this time by God's two Witnesses**, right in His holy city, for three and a half years to anyone who will listen.

Now the Gospel has gone full circle around the world and returned to the very place it began. Even the Witnesses clothing, sackcloth, indicates sorrow and repentance (ancient Jewish custom)! So, here they are, dressed for the occasion, prophesying the true Gospel of the death and resurrection of Jesus Christ as the Savior of the Jews, as well as the whole world to anyone who will accept it.

With the Witnesses' message came the evidence of God's power over the elements, and even death itself! As the Witnesses went around the city proclaiming their message, they had the power to shut off the rain, turn the water into blood, and to scourge the earth with all kinds of plagues as often as they chose to do so. If anyone attempted to accost or injure them, fire poured out of their mouths and consumed them! They couldn't be stopped! No more persecution for preaching the Gospel…the persecutors died!

As the Witnesses proclaimed the Gospel of Christ and the speedy triumph of Christ's kingdom, their worst enemy appeared! More events were about to happen.

Satan, the beast, came up out of the Abyss and conquered the two Witnesses and killed them; yes, killed them!! Satan still has the power to destroy; he has not yet been contained. In all appearances, God's attempt to save the Jews has failed miserably!! In all of God's power to save, Satan has managed to overcome it and destroy God's messengers!! SO, now what??

A worldwide celebration and party started!! The population is overjoyed that these two irritants are gone! The two Witnesses not only pestered the stuffings out of everyone with their messages, they hurt people, caused a draught and muddied their water! The world was GLAD they were dead! They were SO glad that they left their bodies in the street for three and a half days for people to see that they were really dead!

Can you imagine, the news media is all over this! Revelation 11:10 tells us how the whole world reacted to this catastrophic event:

"And those who dwell on the earth will gloat and exult over them and rejoice exceedingly, taking their ease and sending presents to one another, because two Prophets had been such a vexation and trouble and torment to all dwellers of the earth."

The Witnesses had actually finished their purpose and message; **they had proclaimed the Gospel to the Jews and to the whole world one last time,** in the power and force of God, Himself. They were done, except for one last assignment. After three and a half days, God's gift of the breath of life came back to them, they stood up! A strong voice from heaven called them back into God's presence, right before the very eyes of all their enemies!! All of a sudden, the atmosphere changed! The partying stopped dead still! The lies of Satan were revealed, and the people were scared spitless!

As God reclaims His two Witnesses, His great power over the earth is demonstrated once again by the elements; a tremendous earthquake that destroyed part of Jerusalem and killed seven thousand people. FINALLY, those who were left were filled with terror and began to glorify God as they should have all along! **They FINALLY allowed thousands of years of rejection of Jesus and His Gospel to disappear and open their eyes to the Truth; MISSION ACCOMPLISHED!!**

You see, God will do whatever it takes for His Truth to win! He will continue to march right on down the line with His preparation of the earth for the final battle for the souls of mankind.

He is closing in, making the way, eliminating the obstacles, and weakening the enemy for the kill. The second **woe** has now passed, and it is time for the seventh, and last, angel to blow his trumpet.

JESUS Is Now The King Of The Jews

The Jewish nation has been reclaimed right in the beloved city of Jerusalem, and Jesus is FINALLY their king! He has already gathered the "first fruits" of the Jewish nation, those Jews who have already accepted Jesus Christ as their Savior and lived as Christian followers of Christ, and now has won back the WHOLE nation into His kingdom. Satan will not ever again have any influence in their lives, or subject them to persecution for rejecting Christ! God's beloved nation is now permanently safe with Jesus Christ as their King.

The Seventh And Last Trumpet Is Blown

Now, the seventh and final angel blows his trumpet. **The final events of God's preparation, for the ultimate victory over Satan and his evil kingdom, will now begin.** Tremendous voices shouted from heaven to announce the completed dominion of Jesus Christ over all of mankind. Christ's kingdom is now sovereign He has come into possession of it and will reign over it forever in the eternities! All of heaven is rejoicing and praising the Lord for this huge victory of the ages. It is for victory over all the evil that has tainted our world, and the rewarding of the faithful saints and prophets who will live with Him forever.

As heaven is celebrating this huge victory of the dominion of Jesus Christ, the sanctuary in the heavens is opened wide to reveal the ark of God's covenant. As the ark is revealed, the elements, once again, peel out their voices in flashes of lightening, deafening rumblings of loud thunder, earthquakes and a terrific hailstorm. They are not only celebrating the dominion of Jesus Christ, they are excited about the next event!

Event #1 A great sign appeared in heaven, warning of future ominous events.

Please remember that Satan has a fake for everything God has. This event will reveal the true "women" (representing the church) as she appears on the scene to do what she has to do, and how Father God protects her. Later on, the "fake" woman will be revealed in all her evil glory!

The "true woman" represents the church and the righteousness of all those who belong to it. Pay close attention to her attire and her appearance:

- She is clothed with the Sun – the Light of the Gospel of Christ.
- The moon is under her feet – she has the support of the believers who live in the Light.
- She has a tiara of 12 stars on her head – representing the twelve tribes of **Israel**, whom God groomed for

bringing Jesus into the world, and also representing the twelve apostles whom Jesus groomed for bringing the **church** into the world.

She is pregnant with the very soul of the Gospel of Christ that will reclaim those who are willing to embrace the Truth and spread the Gospel of Christ, the ultimate King.

As she cries out in pain of her delivery, the ominous enemy of the church, that old dragon who is Satan himself, appears in heaven. He stations himself directly in front of the approaching birth; a front row seat! He gets so excited about devouring the very birth of the salvation of the believers, that his tail sweeps across the sky, flinging down one-third of the stars to the earth!

Satan should have listened to God when He cursed him in the Garden of Eden, predicting that he may very well bruise the feet of Jesus (in causing His death on the cross), but Jesus would, in turn, bruise Satan's head (that directs his whole agenda of evil). Here, he is stationed right where he thinks he can do the most damage as the "true woman" delivers a

Child Who is destined to shepherd the nations with an iron scepter. Much to Satan's shock and anger, the newly born King of the nations is whisked away to the presence of God and His throne! Not only the newly born King, but the "true woman", herself, fled to the refuge that God had prepared for her to be taken care of while He finished dealing with the dragon. God took them right out from under him, leaving him empty-handed!

Well, that did it for Satan! Now the gloves are off, his quest for overtaking mankind is grossly challenged, and he is going to wage war right there in heaven, to wrench out the very soul of God's Plan! It appears that the biggest deception of Satan is his deceiving of himself!! He has never been able to completely win the war with God, so he must know it is not possible, but he is not about to go down defeated, either.

Event #2 War In Heaven: Satan and his angels against Michael and his angels.

Up until now, Satan has always had a certain amount of freedom to go and come in heaven and on earth, but this time it will be different. Satan has lost his temper against the God of the universe! Now all of heaven has broken loose and fought to cleanse heaven of his presence, and won the battle. There was no place in heaven for Satan or his angels now, so they were literally cast down to earth, never ever to return to heaven. Even heaven has been relieved of his presence. Hallelujah! **No more false accusations of the believers will be made in God's presence!**

Once again, heaven rejoices and proclaims the kingdom rule of Jesus Christ and the salvation of His believers. Now heaven is a completely safe haven for those who have kept the faith, spread the Gospel of Jesus Christ, and some even died because they refused to renounce Jesus as their Savior. Now Jesus has complete authority in heaven without His arch enemy; Satan can no longer contest His authority and dominion! The sacrifice Jesus made on the cross to save mankind is paying off! Those being redeemed from the earth are now coming into God's safe haven in heaven to prepare for the wedding supper of the Lamb.

Look out earth! Satan has been cast out of heaven; he can no longer come and go there. He cannot have the freedom of speech in God's presence, trying to deceive even God,

Himself, by accusing the believers of sins that have already been forgiven! Satan's world is shrinking! Now, he is confined to the earth. In his huge rage, he goes right after the "true woman", the church. But, lo and behold, she is supplied with wings of a giant eagle, to escape to her retreat that God has prepared for her. Satan will never be able to overcome it!!

BUT, Satan will never stop trying until he is forced to stop. Even after all this, he continues to try to overcome the church of Jesus Christ. A huge flood poured from his mouth in hopes of drowning the "true woman", but the ground opened up and consumed the water. Satan will never be able to extinguish the Truth! He will never be able to annihilate the church of Jesus Christ, His Bride! The Bride of Christ IS and WILL BE safe and triumphant, both now and in the end.

Now, in his rage, all the power Satan has left he uses to go after the "true woman's" descendants (the generations of believers). Satan has been confined to the earth, cut off from accusing the church in God's presence. All of his efforts will now be concentrated on anyone who believes, keeps God's commandments and bears witness to the testimony of Jesus

Christ here on earth. Satan is in a permanent rage, is confined to the earth, having only one option left. The earth is about to experience all the ugliness that Satan can muster! The church of Jesus Christ is now beyond his reach in heaven. He now turns on all the unbelievers of the earth to re-group and set up his own kingdom.

Event #3 Satan's Last "Hurrah" Here On Earth

Satan has now been barred from God's presence, cast out of heaven, and confined to the earth with no other place to go except back into the Abyss where he came from! NOW, the earth will brace itself for all the power and meanness, ugliness, violence, death and destruction that Satan and his fallen army of angels can produce! What has angered him the most is that NONE of his efforts have been able to defeat Jesus Christ, or destroy any of His true believers!!

The church of Jesus Christ, the Bride of Christ, is now beyond his reach in heaven. Amazingly, Satan's kingdom of evil still stands! It stands for one reason, and one reason alone: masses of people are still on his side! The stubborn, the rebellious, the ignorant by choice, the selfish and self-centered, the godless, the pagans and everyone else who are truly wicked are still here. **So far, nothing God has done to redeem them has changed their hearts.** They just go right on cursing and discrediting God, and doing what they feel like doing, just like in the days of Noah. Sadly, the history of mankind has been this way through the centuries.

Because the unsaved of the earth have perpetually refused the personal plea of Jesus Christ to change their hearts and be saved by His blood sacrifice He made on the cross, and refused to listen to the Gospel, they are about to experience the power and wrath of Satan right here on earth; **his very last hurrah!** Not only that, **but their opportunities to change are about to end**. By the power of Jesus Christ and Father God, Himself, Satan and all his army of fallen angels have been backed into a corner for the last and final assault on any of mankind. Even as he is funneling ALL his power into his final assault on mankind to ultimately destroy them, Jesus Christ is STILL there trying to change their minds! Even in this monstrous mess of the bitter end, Jesus is STILL holding out for just one more soul who will cry out to Him for salvation in the eternities! Jesus is still here to receive that very last precious soul that would leap out of Satan's stronghold and into His arms forever!!

Now that Satan has been barred from ever entering heaven again, now that he is confined to the earth with nowhere else to go, now that he has been infuriated by his frustrations of not being able to wipe out the church, he is focusing on going after those who obey God and believe the Gospel. He is going to do anything and everything in his power to defeat **each** believer, **on a personal basis**. The gloves are off!! These are some of the actions he will take to try to take YOU down:

- Turn family members against you.
- Cause trouble in your marriage.
- Well-meaning friends will criticize you, even with scripture (like Satan did with Eve in the Garden of Eden, and even Jesus, Himself, when He was tempted by Satan).
- Issues at work.
- Financial challenges.
- Illness.
- Tragedy.
- Etc.

Some of Satan's most effective deceptions he will use:

- The most innocent-looking things, including Bible scriptures taken out of context.
- Things closest to your heart.
- Your weak points.
- Generic things that aren't exactly right or wrong.

We are in a point in time, like never before, where Satan will concentrate on **ruining you personally; yes YOU! He has nothing to lose except YOU!** You have a monstrous, powerful, personal enemy that is concentrating on defeating and destroying you any way he can. God knows that, so, right here in the middle of it all, **Jesus, Himself, instructs you and me in HOW to have the power to overcome and win.** Revelation 12:11 tells us exactly how to **outsmart and overcome** every single challenge Satan accosts you and me with:

*"And they have overcome (conquered) by means of the **blood of the Lamb** and **their testimony**, for they did not love and cling to life even when faced with death."*

The only way to defeat Satan in your own life is to:

- GET SERIOUS!
- Know your enemy – 50% of winning the battle for your soul.
- Keep your eyes on the CROSS – the reason for it all.
- Tell others about the Gospel – Jesus told you to.
- Keep God's spiritual and moral commandments and live every day of your life for Christ no matter what.

There has been enough horrors in this world for the last 2,000 years: unspeakable tragedies, every conceivable atrocity imaginable (such as the holocaust), genocide in countries like Uganda, abortions that have killed millions of innocent babies, and on and on. We've all had enough, but, unfortunately, the worst is yet to come. The world has not experienced all of God's end-time events. **But one thing is different now:**

Satan and his army of fallen angels have been permanently thrown out of heaven **to the earth** with no other place to go.

SO, here he is, right here in our faces! Since he cannot go into heaven to falsely accuse believers, in his fury, he decidedly come directly after the church. When God's power, and even the earth itself protected the church from Satan's grasp in its birth, Satan was enraged even more, and vowed war on anyone keeping the commandments and giving testimony to the Gospel of Jesus Christ. That means **you and me** if we are believers in Jesus Christ!!

Now that Satan is confined here, in all his false glory, he is quickly getting ready to put the pressure on to mankind to take our eyes off Jesus Christ and on to his own spectacular evil deeds. He is revving up to show people his power so that the unsaved will finally have something **visible and spectacular to woo them to worship him.**

Remember that Satan has a "fake" for everything God has; he is a master at holograms! He is a master at making things look genuine, even though they are pure deception. You will recognize at least two major "fakes" as Satan is setting up for his last "hurrah", the last holocaust, his last deception of the people of the earth. If you are not already a believer in Jesus

Christ, you will not be able to stand up against this worldwide push to entrap and destroy mankind. Even as Satan is making his miraculous comeback, you will see Jesus STILL holding out for that one soul who will repent and believe in Him!

Right in the middle of all the chaos and carnage, Jesus says,

'Behold, I am going to come like a thief! Blessed (happy, to be envied) is he who stays awake (alert) and guards his clothes, so that he may not be naked and [have the shame of being] seen exposed." Rev.16:20

As Jesus continues to show the apostle John the miraculous, spectacular and overwhelming global show of all of Satan's death-grip on the unsaved of the earth, Satan creates three major spectacles.

Spectacle #1 The Beast From The Sea

As John is looking to see what is next, he sees a beast coming up out of the sea. The beast appears to be a leopard with seven heads and ten horns, paws like a bear and a mouth like a lion. He is plastered with all kinds of blasphemous words and names directed toward Jehovah God. One of his heads appeared to have a death stroke. This death wound was caused by the death and resurrection of Jesus Christ, predicted In Genesis when God placed a curse on him, saying that he would wound Jesus' heel, but Jesus would wound his head.

As the people of the earth observed in awe and amazement, the dragon (Satan) allows this new beast to have his power and dominion and to sit on his own throne. As the dragon gave the new beast all his power and false glory, all of a sudden the blasphemous beast's head **wound** was **healed**!!! All the page in amazement and admiration! They not only paid homage to the beast, but paid worship and homage to the dragon for producing the beast and for giving him power and authority.

The Beast From The Sea Captivating The People of The Earth

The beast was also given the power of speech and the authority to do whatever he willed to do. The very **first** thing he did was to blaspheme and slander the God of the heavens as well as everyone living in heaven (out of his reach!). He wanted to make sure no one looked to God for anything! The **second** thing he did was exercise his authority to go directly after the believers and overcome their efforts to effectively testify with the Gospel.

Now that the beast has seemingly disabled God's authority and the testimony of Jesus Christ in the minds of the masses (the "madding crowd"), the unsaved, they are ALL in his grip so he can finish his dastardly saga of deceit and entrapment.

Revelation 13:8 reveals just who these people are,

And all the inhabitants of the earth will bow down in admiration and pay him homage, ***everyone whose name has not been recorded in the Book of Life of the Lamb*** *that was slain from the foundation of the world."*

They could have had their name in the Book of Life by repenting and believing in Jesus Christ! It's that simple!

In spite of these diabolical, evil events, where Satan, the dragon, and the leopard beast are creating this deception, heaven is STILL wide open and Jesus Christ is STILL offering salvation to anyone who will repent and accept salvation!

Spectacle #2 The Second Beast Appears

Lo and behold! Satan isn't done yet! Here comes another beast! This one has come from the land (instead of the sea), having horns like a lamb but roars like a dragon. His purpose is to perpetrate and participate in the power of the first beast, whose death wound was healed. This new beast was powerful and seemed to perform miracles, even making fire fall from the sky. He was so effective that all the unsaved of the earth were deceived; Satan's seeming victory!

The new beast commanded the people to erect a statue in the likeness of the beast. He even arranged for the statue to actually talk! He further commanded the people to worship the statue or be killed.

Spectacle #3 The Mark Of The Beast

Now that the dragon, who is none other than Satan, himself, and the two beasts have managed to frighten, seduce and deceive the people and kill all who refuse to do what they command, he is getting ready to "seal the deal" by marking his territory permanently.

He compels ALL people, no matter what their status in life is, to submit to having a tattooed inscription on the right hand and/or the forehead. Furthermore, one could not buy or sell anything unless they had the tattoo of the beast.

The tattoo was probably the same as the calculated number of the beast that Revelation says is the number of a man, "666". This tattoo is a "fake" to replace the "mark of God" that was given by the Holy Spirit to the believers in Jesus Christ. Those whose names are already written in the Lamb's Book of Life are safe and protected from the "fake" mark that Satan is giving.

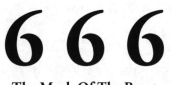

666

The Mark Of The Beast

The Solid Power Of Heaven and The Lamb Show Victory

Even as Satan has mustered up every diabolical power he has access to, killed those refusing to worship the beast, and marking those who keep following him, Jesus Christ is STILL able to save anyone willing to repent and believer in Him! At this pointy in time, it is not likely that anyone will change their mind; they have been dooped by all the wonders Satan has performed so far, and marked them for the "kill", their final destruction.

Jesus knows one thing, this is the very last hurrah for Satan. Soon, time will be no more, and heaven's doors will close forever to these unsaved people. Jesus created mankind (John 1:1, 2) to be with Him, NOT to be doomed with Satan and his crew! Even now, when it is next to impossible for these people to make a change, Jesus is STILL offering His invitation of salvation from sin and doom, and a home with Him forever!

As Satan is seen ruling the earth with his mega-power, over all the unsaved of the earth, the apostle John records another scene in heaven. A scene of those who have overcome and had victory over Satan's stranglehold on mankind. In chapter seven of Revelation, when Jesus had opened the sixth seal of the scroll, the angels that held back the destructive winds, were instructed to hold back any harm to the earth while God's people were sealed with the **seal of God; these are those people**.

In chapter seven, 144,000 Jewish people were sealed, as well as a mass of people too numerous to count. **All of them, together, are protected from any harm that is coming to the earth.** In fact, they have been taken to heaven where they are attired in white robes, already serving Father God, and Jesus Christ the Son, day and night. In this chapter, he gives us a priceless view of heaven:

"...they are now before the throne of God and serve Him day and night in His sanctuary; and He, Who is sitting on the throne, will protect and spread His tabernacle over them and shelter them with His presence. They will hunger no more, neither thirst

anymore; neither shall the sun smite them, nor any scorching heat. For the Lamb Who is in the midst of the throne will be their Shepherd, and He will guide them to the springs of the waters of Life, and God will wipe away every tear from their eyes."

These are those who will never again be challenged with the wiles of Satan! They have made it safely home to be with Father God and Jesus Christ forever. Now, after many events of preparation from heaven, and the very last rule of Satan is taking place, with its iron grip on the unsaved of the earth, the 144,000 and all of those who have the seal of God inscribed on their forehead, appear with Jesus Christ on Mount Zion, accompanied by a huge, expansive, unified voice sounding like harpists. These are the same people that we first learned about in chapter seven. They are called the "first fruits redeemed from the earth for God and the Lamb". They are singing a new song that no other beings could learn.

One Last Chance To Hear The Gospel and Be Saved

As the Lamb, and the untouchable redeemed from the earth, are standing on Mount Zion, another angel is flying in midair with the eternal Gospel to tell all the inhabitants of the earth, every race, tribe, language and people, its story of salvation. He cried with a mighty voice:

Revere God and give Him glory (honor and praise in worship) for the hour of His judgment has arrived. Fall down before Him, give Him the homage and adoration and worship Him Who created heaven and earth, the sea and springs of water."

The last warning, to those who have been following Satan, is given by a second angel with a mighty voice for all to hear,

"Whomever pays homage to the beast and his statue, and permits the beast's stamp (mark, inscription) to be put on his forehead or on his hand, he too shall drink of the wine of God's indignation and wrath, poured out undiluted into the cup of His anger; and shall be tormented with fire and brimstone in the presence of the holy angels and in the presence of the Lamb. And the smoke of their torment ascends forever and ever, and they have no respite (no pause, no intermission, no rest, no peace) day or night – these who pay homage to the beast and to his imager and whoever receives the stamp of his name upon him." Rev.14:9

Along with the last warning comes a **voice of reassurance from heaven directed to anyone who may still choose salvation:**

"Blessed (and happy) are the dead from now on who die in the Lord! Yes, blessed and happy, says the Spirit, that they may rest from their labors, for their works (deeds) do follow them!"

Jesus knows that every single human was created by Him to match Himself and Father God. The only thing missing from unsaved mankind, in their independence, is making a personal choice to line up with their Creator. Jesus also knows what will happen to anyone who will not choose to be redeemed by God. **Mankind was never meant to be tormented in the place where Satan will be eternally punished;** it was meant only for Satan and those angels that followed him into his rebellion against God. Jesus desperately desires to redeem every single person He died for. He is willing to forgive anyone who is willing to repent of his/her sins and accept salvation. Just so you know, **salvation is unique to mankind; Satan and his angels will never have that privilege!** This is the **last call** from Jesus Christ to His beloved human race, the ones He gave His life for.

The Last Harvest Of Souls
From The Earth

Satan's evil kingdom has come to a climax with all the power he can muster. He has successfully claimed masses of people who have followed his fake miracles and wonders, and taken his mark of ownership.

Jesus Christ has come to Mount Zion with the 144,000 Jewish believers and hundreds of millions of believers who are now safe from evil. There is to be one more harvest of souls from the earth before Father God finishes His wrath toward evil and destroys Satan's kingdom completely and forever, never to harm anyone again.

This last harvest has come in two parts, the harvest of the brave souls who have actually recognized the Truth and accepted Jesus as their Savior, and those that refused to change.

The First Harvest

A white cloud appears, with someone sitting on it, that looks like the Son of Man with a gold crown on his head. He has a sickle in his hand. An angel comes out of the temple in heaven, and shouts in a loud voice to the Man with the sickle,

"Put in your sickle to reap, for the hour has arrived to gather the harvest, for the earth's crop is fully ripened." He Who was sitting on the cloud swung His sickle and the earth's crop was harvested.

This harvest from the earth is the very last of those who have opened their hearts to God's Truth, repented and accepted Jesus Christ as their Savior, rejecting the kingdom of Satan. This harvest of souls is the last of mankind that has left Satan's domination to be saved from destruction. Jesus has now taken the very last repentant soul that will ever be taken from the earth.

The Second Harvest

Another angel comes out of the temple in heaven with a sharp sickle. The angel, with authority over the fire on the altar of God, called with a loud cry to the angel with the sharp sickle, *"Put forth your sickle and reap the fruitage of the vine of the earth, for its grapes are entirely ripe."* The angel with the sharp sickle swung it on the earth and gathered the vintage of the earth and cast it into the winepress of God's indignation and wrath. Revelation 14:20 is shocking beyond belief!! The horror of God's winepress is this,

"And the grapes in the winepress were trodden outside the city, and blood poured from the winepress reaching as high as the horse's bridles for a distance of 1600 stadia (about 200 miles)."

This is the harvest that Jesus was frantically trying to warn mankind to avoid; the harvest He never wanted to be made. Unfortunately, this harvest is for people who have continued to maximize their rebellion against God with their evil-drenched lives, until their lives are fixed and matured in it. These are the ones who will never change, never accept Jesus Christ. As we will discover later on, this group of people are not ALL the people left on earth. They ARE the ones who have matured in their rebellious lives they have chosen to live; they have lived it on purpose, in it's entirety, and now they are ready for harvest.

God's Final Wrath Here On Earth

Believe it or not, there is still a bare chance for people to repent and believe in Jesus Christ! Unfortunately, there is no one left on earth that has repented and changed, so the chances are very slim that anyone else will make the changes; even so, it IS still possible. There is very little time left, and it is the very last time that anyone will have a chance to repent. Even as the chances for redemption are about to end, Jesus Christ is STILL offering hope to the lost! What a Savior we have!!

Satan STILL has a stranglehold on the masses who have not repented, and have taken Satan's mark of identity in their forehead or hand. The dragon (Satan), the leopard beast and the talking statue are still holding them captivated. None of the events that have happened have changed their minds; Satan's power is still in place. Even so, there is STILL a chance for any of them to change their minds to repent and accept God's salvation from it all.

This a breath-holding moment in time!! Will they or won't they?? Will anyone see it?? Will anyone be wise instead of foolish?? Is their God-created brain seared over with a hot iron?? Doesn't their "gut feeling" tell them anything?? Don't they understand that God has ALWAYS been more powerful than Satan?? Do they think Satan has a heaven waiting for them?? Don't they understand they are trading their birthright for a time of evil pleasure?? Then what??

This is day, this is the time, this is the very LAST chance they will EVER have, in all of eternity, to change their minds. **Satan is about to lose ALL his power; his followers will pay the ultimate price.**

Now, as the seven angels distribute the **last** of the plagues, the **last** of God's vengeance against evil, (can you believe it?) **Jesus is STILL listening for that one last soul who will cry out and repent!!** Those souls that have come out victorious from the beast and his statue, and from receiving his tattoo, are now worshipping in the presence of God, singing the song of Moses and the song of the Lamb. They declare His just and righteous judgments that have been known and displayed for all to see.

An Ominous Sign Appears In Heaven

As John looked, the doors of the sanctuary of the testimony in heaven were thrown open, and he saw seven angels, dressed in white with golden sashes, bringing out seven plagues. They were given seven bowls full of the wrath and indignation of the God of the universe, Who lives forever in the eternity of the eternities.

Can you even begin to comprehend the horror that Father God has to face now?? He has been trying to retrieve His creation for over six thousand years; ever since the fall of mankind into sin in the Garden. His Plan has now gone through all the necessary phases to this ultimate point in time when He must separate the righteous, as well as all of heaven and earth, from ALL evil. EVIL must be permanently contained forever, never again being able to have any influence over anyone.

The wrath of God is against EVIL itself, so His wrath must be completely fulfilled. It is now time to execute sentence on all who have chosen not to repent and be saved. What an earth-shaking, gut-wrenching, sad day for the Father of all creation!! Because it is such a horrific day for Him, you will notice that, as the angels pour out each final wrath, they reassure our sad Father God that His judgments are righteous and correct. Be reassured that not a single righteous person will receive any of God's wrath; it is solely for the **unsaved**.

As God is about to pour out all the rest of His wrath on the unsaved masses, the sanctuary in heaven is so full of smoke from His glory and might and power, that no one could go into it until the seven angels had finished their assignment. A mighty voice from the temple told the seven angels to go and empty out their bowls of God's final wrath on the earth.

Angel #1 went and emptied his bowl on the earth, and foul and painful ulcers came upon the people who had taken the tattoo of the beast and worshipped his statue.

Angel #2 emptied his bowl on the sea, turning it into blood like a corpse (thick, corrupt, ill-smelling and disgusting), and every living thing in the sea died.

Angel #3 emptied his bowl into the rivers and the springs of water, and they turned into blood.

At this point in time, the angel of the waters declared, *"Righteous are You in these decisions and judgments, You Who are and were, O Holy One! Because they have poured out the blood of your people and the prophets, and You have given them blood to drink. Such is their due [they deserve it!]"*

Then came a cry from the altar of God, a voice agreeing with God's judgments, *"Yes, Lord God the Omnipotent, Your judgments (sentences, decisions) are true and just and righteous!"*

Angel #4 emptied out his bowl upon the sun, and it was permitted to burn (scorch) humanity with fierce, glowing heat (fire). People were severely burned by the fiery heat and they **reviled and blasphemed God,** Who had control of these plagues, and they **did not repent** of their sins [felt no regret, contrition and compunction for their waywardness], **refusing to amend their ways to give Him glory.**

Understand the significance of this response of the people; Jesus Christ is STILL open to their repentance, even though there is not much hope for these false worshippers. SO, the bowls of God's wrath continue to be poured out. God's wrath moves right on in to the **source of their rebellion**.

Angel #5 emptied his bowl directly on the **throne of the beast**, plunging his kingdom into darkness, disabling the power and the deceiving glory of it. The confusion and panic that followed plunged the people into horrible reactions, like gnawing their tongues, causing excruciating pain and distress.

Can you imagine?? Their whole world has been turned into a huge nightmare, a crucible of chaos and pain; a little taste of Hell, itself! The true God they have ignored, thinking He was just some wimpy figment of someone's imagination, is actually alive and well! Yet, in spite of their rebellion, He is STILL willing to accept their repentance! Unfortunately, none are willing to repent. Even though they realize it is the true God Who is dismantling Satan's kingdom of evil and punishing those who choose to follow him. This is what Revelation 16:11 says they did instead: *"And **blasphemed the God** of heaven because of their anguish and their ulcers, and they **did not deplore their wicked deeds or repent** for what they had done!"*

This was their very **last chance** at making a change, their very **last chance** to repent and accept Jesus Christ as their Savior. As the last two angels empty their bowls, the scene changes to preparation for Armageddon, the final confrontation between good and evil.

Angel #6 poured out his bowl on the mighty Euphrates River, and its water was dried up to make ready a road for the coming of the kings of the East, from the rising sun.

Now the true identity of Satan's cohorts are revealed. John sees three disgusting spirits in the form of frogs leaping from the mouths of all three of the evil leaders; the dragon, the beast and the false prophet. Kind of reminds me of some movies I have seen! These evil, disgusting spirits are **demons** that perform wonders and miracles. The masses have been duped and trapped by this power of Satan all along! Satan still has these people under his power, so he turns his attention toward his final confrontation with God Almighty.

These evil demons continue their evil activities by going all over the world to the leaders and rulers, gathering them together for war on the Great Day of the God Almighty. The demons have now gathered the leaders and the rulers of the world to a place called **Armageddon** in the Hebrew language. This will be the turning point for Satan's evil kingdom.

Almighty God has completed all His preparations, for this very time in history, and He is now ready to put an end to Satan's rule and influence over mankind.

Angel #7 pours out his bowl in the air. A mighty voice came out of the sanctuary of heaven from the very throne of God, saying,

"IT IS DONE! IT IS ALL ACCOMPLISHED, IT HAS COME!"

God almighty has backed Satan into a corner, taking all the wind out of his sales, de-throning him in public, revealing the truth about his power and his wonders to be demon-generated, leaving him nothing but the reality of his weaknesses!! Every element and event of God's preparations have been successfully accomplished!

Now the elements of the earth and sky rejoice and erupt into an unprecedented, all out show of God's forces:

- Lightening flashes
- Loud rumblings
- Peals of thunder
- A tremendous, severe earthquake so widespread it went all around the world. Never has there been an earthquake like it ever before.
- Jerusalem was broken into three sections
- The cities of the world fell
- Every island fled and no mountain was found
- 50lb. hail stones fell from the sky on to the **unsaved** people and they **blasphemed God** for the great torture.

Now God is ready to take Satan out, to a complete end to all his evil influence around the world. John is about to be privileged to witness the spectacular and complete destruction of evil. Evil will never again be able to touch or affect anything in God's world for all of eternity!

The Final Destruction
Of Babylon Begins

Babylon has always been, and still is, considered the epitome of evil as soon as the word "Babylon" is spoken! God has chosen this name to represent sin because of its history. The original city of Babylon was built by an incredible man by the name of Nimrod. Nimrod built a whole empire that included Babylon and Nineveh. The infamous story of the Tower of Babel originated here. Babylon was one of the very first big cities here on earth. In fact, Babylon was the richest and most powerful city that has ever been built in all of history; they literally ruled the known world.

They got so rich and powerful that they soon turned from worshipping God, to being their own gods of power and glory, worshipping the "created" rather than the Creator. The world has had a problem with this very practice all the way through history, even to this day. Worshipping the "created" rather than the Creator has been a huge and diverse malady of mankind ever since. In our day and time, it is "Mother Earth" and mankind wanting to be self-sufficient without having to be beholden to a "higher being".

As the Babylonian empire grew, and became the strongest nation in the world, their aspirations were to **BE** God! That is why they decided to build the Tower of Babel (Babylon). They convinced themselves that they could build the tower high enough to **reach God and take over heaven itself**! That is why Jehovah God confused their language into many languages, so that they couldn't understand each other and work together anymore. Diverse languages became one of God's ways of controlling His errant creation, mankind. Down through the ages, Babylon has become the standard that represents the evil practices that were and are, and will continue to be in the world as we know it.

Here in the book of Revelation, God has reserved the infamous Babylon to represent **ALL of the evil that has ever been in the world.** Now it is time to call her to her final judgment and demise, along with her perpetrator, Satan. Satan is represented here as a huge red beast that the "Prostitute Babylon" is sitting upon; the very beast that has caused all the evil in our world in the first place!

The beast and the prostitute Babylon

Unfortunately, all those who have made a decision to continue following the wicked ways of the beast will get worse. In II Timothy 3:13, Paul tells Timothy that, *"wicked men and imposters will go from bad to worse, deceiving and leading astray others and being deceived and led astray themselves"*. These are the very people Jesus Christ is trying to reach, here in Revelation, before it is too late!! Jesus is trying His best to unravel the sticky spider web that has wrapped itself around them to disable their salvation! Anyone of them can STILL escape while there is still time, while Jesus is still here, willing to "unravel" Satan's hold on them. Jesus Christ is the only friend with the power to rescue that person who repents and follows Him.

As God prepares to reveal, unravel and eliminate Satan's entire evil empire, the world goes on as usual; much like in the days of Noah and of Sodom. People have been living their everyday lives as usual, going to work, coming home, eating food, playing games, sleeping, etc. Most have been oblivious to anything God is doing, most are ignorant of the Bible, and just go on with life and hope for the best. Those of us who know and believe the Truth, can only look on in compassion and pray that they will open their eyes to God's Truth and receive the Gospel before it is too late.

Believers need to have the same sense of urgency as Jesus, Himself, has right up to the end of time as we know it; as it unfolds right before our eyes! WE are the carriers of the Gospel that can save them!

John has now been instructed to write down this whole event for us. God has now finished with ALL the preparations for Him to take down Satan's whole, worldwide network of evil. It is time for John to sit in the grandstand to observe and record all that is about to happen. One of the seven angels, that had emptied his bowl of God's wrath in the preparation, has taken John away in the Spirit into a wilderness areas where he could plainly observe this huge event; the destruction of this **empire of evil** that has so cleverly intoxicated the unsaved of the world, and robbed them of their eternal salvation.

As John observes this **final event of victory over evil**, a spectacular, but ominous, scene appears. The angel, that has escorted John to this scene of doom, explains to him exactly what he is looking at. He said to John,

*"I will show you the doom (sentence, judgment) of the **great harlot** who is seated on many waters, she with whom the rulers of the earth have joined in prostitution (idolatry) and with the wine of whose immorality (idolatry)the inhabitants of the earth have become intoxicated."*

John is about to witness what we all wish for, the demise of Satan's power to entrap, deceive and destroy God's creation. Here in Revelation, Jesus Christ is making sure we can all read "the end of the story" before it is too late to repent and accept salvation. This spectacular event unveils ALL evil as it really is, all the real ugliness of Satan's whole false kingdom. It shows the eternal power of Jehovah God to make things right, and imprison Satan and confine him to his own space forever and ever.

Babylon The Great Prostitute

As John looked, he saw a woman seated upon a red beast who is covered with blasphemous names; he had seven heads and ten horns. Remember him from the last event?? Same guy. The woman sitting on the beast was all decked out in the finest clothes and jewelry she could use. Her robe was purple (indicating royalty) and scarlet and bedecked with gold, precious stones and pearls, and she held a golden cup in her hand that was full of her accursed offenses, and the filth of her lewdness and vice. She is drunk with the blood of the martyrs and all the people she has slaughtered.

She has a mysterious name inscribed on her forehead with a symbolic meaning: BABYLON THE GREAT, **the mother of prostitutes** (idolatries) and the filth and atrocities and abominations of the earth. Her ID is on her forehead, just like the people that followed the beast and had his mark on their foreheads!

She is the epitome of every sin that has ever been committed in all of time here on earth. This what the reality of sin looks like. She has spun her sticky web in every aspect of daily life here on earth; with the nation's leaders, the world's commerce, buying and selling everywhere, the economy of nations, wealth and luxuries of business men living high off the hog because they have been "in bed" with her, participating in her evil ways.

Her evil ways include every single sin that has ever been committed down through time! According to Revelation 17 and 18, every single aspect of the world's economy is all wrapped up and entangled in her evil web, including every:

- Scam
- Unfair business practice
- Inflated economy
- Economic crash
- Deceit and lies
- Murders and heinous attacks, war
- Disappointment and depression
- Divorce and ill feelings

- Thieves
- Abandonment
- Sexual vice
- Tears
- Diseases and afflictions

…and the list is endless. She has successfully lured the masses with her finery, her wealth and her lewdness. Revelation 18:3, 5 says,

"For all nations have drunk the wine of her passionate unchastity, and the leaders and rulers of the earth have joined with her in committing fornication (idolatry), and the businessmen of the earth have become rich with the wealth her excessive luxury and wantonness. Her iniquities (crimes and transgressions) are piled up as high as heaven, and God has remembered her wickedness and crimes [and called her up for settlement]."

What John is seeing is the huge and final picture of sin and evil as it really is; all the filth and ugliness that she has caused to permeate the world. Every atrocity that has ever happened, such as the death of Jesus, Hitler's crimes, slavery with all its injustices, all the horrors of war; **this is Babylon The Great Prostitute**.

The beast she is sitting on is the very same beast that the dragon, Satan, used to deceive the masses, the very one to whom he gave his power and authority, the very one who demanded his followers to take his mark, his tattoo, in their hand or forehead; yes, the very one who caused the evil statue to talk; He's the very one who killed people who refused to worship him and receive his mark. SO, here he is carrying the Great Prostitute to her **doom!** This is one last look at what they have created for all the unsaved, stubborn and rebellious people of the world!

You understand now, WHY God has saved Babylon to represent the triumphant end of ALL the evil that has plagued the earth since Adam and Eve. The nations, the masses of people have belligerently, rebelliously and stubbornly continued to allow Satan to rule their lives. Now they are getting ready to witness, and be shocked by, the **abrupt end of Satan's whole evil system, leaving them virtually mid-stream and helpless** to do anything about it; their lives ruined forever.

The economy of the whole world has depended on Babylon. Because the people and the merchants have built their business and their success on the greed for luxury and riches, rather than giving God the glory for making it happen for them, the whole network is going down. Jesus told a parable about two men who build their houses; the wise man built his house on a firm foundation, the other man built his house on the sand. When the storms (of life) came, the house built on the unstable sand was washed away, but the house built on a firm foundation {Jesus Christ) withstood the storms.

Babylon's kingdom is built on the foundation of the "sand" of greed and sinful practices, leaving God out of the picture; God's kingdom is built on the foundation of perfect righteousness that stands forever.

The business men and the people who have allowed themselves to be deceived into false success and vain living, have built the structure of their lives on the sand that is not stable. It didn't get that way overnight! Most vain living comes about over time, little by little, slipping away from Father God's ways into their own ways; depending on their own reasoning rather than God's wisdom. The Bible says that people have no excuse for being ignorant of God because His creation is all around us, bigger than we are; we, who are made in the likeness of God in the first place!

Understand that these people "look good and smell good" in the eyes of the world, they feel like they have done well, been successful, "arrived". What they have **really done** is leave God and His principles out of the picture and in the dust, going right on down the broad and beautiful highway to their doom. They are the very same crowd that King Solomon talks about in Proverbs: the madding crowd, oblivious to where they will end up.

There is one major reality of life that unsaved people seem to ignore until it hits them right squarely in the face, and that is, death. Death is a reality that no one can ignore; it's going to happen! You would think that the positive belief of living with God in the eternities would motivate most people, but the truth is, people look for every conceivable answer they can dig up rather than be excited about living in unprecedented luxury with no pain or tears, actually seeing our loved ones again, actually seeing Jesus Christ Who has saved us from our sins, plus all the things God has in store for us that we can't even comprehend!! Go figure!!

But this is the very thing that Satan does not want anyone to enjoy! He knows very well that Jesus' home in heaven is still open to anyone and everyone who will repent and accept Jesus as Savior. Satan can no longer go there; of course he doesn't want you to go there either! That is the goal of all he does, that is, to destroy your chances of going there and living there forever. He makes dead-end avenues look like beautiful highways to the unsaved people of the world, because he knows where they go – nowhere!

All the people of the world, who have gotten caught up in Satan's evil network, are about to be left "holding the bag"; they are at the **end** of the dead-end avenues they have been traveling on throughout their lives. They are about to be left with no way to recover their losses. Their true leader, the Great Prostitute, is about to be called up for her final judgment by the Creator of the universe. All in one day she will be completely destroyed, never to do damage again. This is the day of **her judgment, recorded in Revelation 18:5-8,**

"For her iniquities (crimes and transgressions) are piled up as high as heaven, and God has remembered her wickedness and crimes [and called them up for settlement]. Repay to her what she herself has paid [to others] and double [her doom] in accordance with what she has done. Mix a double portion for her in the cup she mixed [for others]. To the degree that she glorified herself, and revealed in her wantonness [living deliciously and luxuriously], to that measure impose on her torment and anguish and tears and mourning, so shall her plagues (afflictions and calamities) come back upon her in a single day; pestilence and sorrow and anguish and famine, and she shall be utterly consumed (burned up with fire), for great is the Lord Who judges her."

You may remember the notorious account of Sodom and Gomorrah in the Old Testament in Abraham's day. They were so debauched, and horrifyingly wicked, that God rained down fire and brimstone on them and destroyed them; Father God means "business"! He will never ever tolerate evil and wickedness without repentance or recompense. The whole book of Revelation is about the exact same thing; **reward or recompense.**

Another thing God always does is give you plenty of warning. God has allowed His sinful creation to go on down the road of sin and debauchery for over 6,000 years, and now it is time to put a permanent end to what has caused all the devastation. God's Word says that He is not slack concerning His promises to bring mankind back to perfection, but has been waiting longer than He wanted to so more people will change their mind and repent, so they can live with Him forever. You know He must be dreading this bitter end, for **when He brings the hammer down, it will be the end of mankind's chance for salvation.** God will no longer be able to offer salvation to anyone.

Now it is time for Babylon to represent the ultimate annihilation of all evil that has ever been, all the evil that has caused all of mankind's alienation from God. **This is it! This is the time for the demise of Satan's network of evil**, time for Satan to be all done scamming the world God created! God is not slack and He is not slow; Babylon is going down suddenly, all in one day. The world is about to have permanent relief from all evil.

Suddenly, the hammer comes crashing down! Babylon is annihilated right in the middle of "life as usual"! Suddenly, life is not "usual" anymore! The whole world is caught off guard; the whole commercial world in particular! Every business person in the whole world has been left "holding the bag" right in the middle of their business day, right where they stood! NOTHING is what is was, nothing is working, ALL is chaos!!

The ships on the sea, the stores in the mall, the gas stations, all restaurants, the planes in the air, all the traffic; every aspect of daily life! The smoke from Babylon's demise is visible all over the whole world. **Every single person who has participated in her commercial web is all done, never to be part of it ever again.**

As Babylon is left smoking in the dust of her own destruction, every single person involved in her economy is suddenly out of business! Every bit of business created through her fraudulent system is all done! Not only all done, but left "holding the bag" with no way to fix it! Not only is Babylon all done, so is the economy that has been based on her evil ways. In Revelation 18:9-19, it gives us a clear picture of the aftermath of Babylon's destruction that caught the whole worldwide economy by surprise.

- The rulers and leaders of the earth who joined in her evil ways will weep and lament.
- The earth's business men will weep and grieve because no one is left to buy their wares.
- The retail dealers who did business with them will weep and grieve.
- Transportation businessmen weep and grieve over their.

While Babylon's smoke is still rising, and all those involved in her schemes are panicking and wringing their hands at their helpless and permanent plight, a single powerful angel makes a big final announcement about Babylon, using a demonstration of HOW final this destruction is. He hurled a heavy millstone into the sea, crying:

*"With such violence shall Babylon the great city be hurled down
to destruction and shall never be found…and in her was found
the blood of prophets and of saints and of all those who have been
slain (slaughtered) on the earth." Rev.18:18, 24*

The aftermath of the sudden destruction of Babylon has
left a huge mess all over the world!! The world view at this
time is not pretty! The whole economic system is gone; no
one is doing business as usual. Everyday life has come to a
screeching halt! Panic and horror have set in! It's time to "pay
the fiddler". The Bible teaches us that the only thing that will
survive in the end is the Word of God, which is TRUTH.
There is NO truth in Satan's system in his false kingdom.
These people are still alive, reaping the results of the damage
their choices have produced.

As the people who are left on the earth are bemoaning their
plight, there is a mighty shout of a great crowd in heaven
celebrating the unprecedented victory of God over evil! From
now on, they can praise the mighty God Who has saved them
from disaster forever!

Jesus' whole purpose of recording these spectacular events in a book for us is so that everyone will have a better choice and have a better ending for themselves. Jesus is here giving **everyone** a chance to know future events to see what will happen in the end of time as we know it. It gives us all a chance to pick which side we want to be on. It gives us a chance to identify our enemy and see who he really is, and what is going to happen to him and all those who choose to remain on his side. It gives everyone a chance to **leave** Satan's kingdom, and join Jesus Christ in His triumph over it all!

An angel appeared to make a final announcement about Babylon. Father God wants to make sure that all of heaven and earth know that there will never be another Babylon with all of its vices and wickedness. The wickedness represented by the infamous name of "Babylon" includes ALL wickedness. That is why God had to destroy HER wickedness; simultaneously taking away all Satan has to work with. Now, he has nothing to go on, nothing to use to deceive anyone with, he has been separated from all of his devices; now he can be taken out!

All the preparations God has made has made it possible to single him out and confine him. When he has been confined, the world will be free of his evil influence. All those who are left on earth will be at the mercy of all the events that are about to take place.

John was so overwhelmed by this revelation that he fell prostrate in front of the angel messenger to worship; in awe of all that had taken place. The angel quickly ordered him to refrain from doing that, exclaiming that he, too, was a servant, along with us, and we should worship only God. The angel explains it in a nutshell:

"I am only another servant with you and your brethren who have the testimony borne by Jesus Christ. Worship God! For the substance of the Truth revealed by Jesus is the spirit of all prophecy [the vital breath, the inspiration of all inspired preaching and interpretation of the divine will and purpose, including mine and yours]:. Rev. 19:10

All of the monumental and wondrous events, John has been shown, are almost more than he can take in. He has been filled up with spectacles never before been seen or heard!! He is beholding the actual **reality of his lifetime of faith in God and Jesus Christ**, being given the exclusive privilege of **seeing what the death, burial and resurrection of Jesus Christ has made possible for all of mankind**; wiping out evil and allowing God's believers to live in perfect peace forever!

Jesus wants us to be sure and be there with Him! He is there now, preparing for you and me to be there! That is the very reason He is here with John, revealing to us all the events of the end of the ages, and giving us His **personal invitation** to every person. He wants you there at His marriage feast! Once you get there, you will never have to leave; you are home!

Now that Satan's network of evil has been destroyed, nothing is organized anymore, chaos and bewilderment reigns on the earth, there are more events that must take place before our world is restored to perfection. You remember that there are still masses of people on the earth that were left "holding the bag" when Satan's kingdom collapsed. They have nothing left now but their punishment for allowing themselves to be immersed in Satan's false economic system. **None have faith in Jesus Christ.**

Those that have accepted Jesus as their Savior, and are already in heaven praising the mighty God Who has saved them, have lived by their FAITH in a God they cannot see, a **God that has stored up their faith** in heaven where it is safe, along with the TESTIMONY of the Gospel. **Our faith, together with the testimony of Jesus, is the VICTORY that overcomes the world!!**

Understanding FAITH is a challenge to us all. The Bible describes faith as the substance of things hoped for and the reality of things not visible to us with our earthly eyes; that makes it hard! Believing in something you cannot see makes it difficult to grab on to the concept of FAITH, yet, God bases His whole Plan for us on this FAITH. Jesus once told His apostles that miracles cannot happen without people having FAITH. In fact, not much of our active Christian life can happen without this faith. Faith is something that must grow continually, just like our bodies. It must grow through thick and thin, through all of life's hardships and disappointments.

This faith is what will get you where you want to go, that is, to heaven to live with God forever!

In the book of Hebrews, it describes the faith of many outstanding characters of the Old Testament. It also describes them as sitting in the "grandstands" cheering us on as we try to follow their footsteps in our journey of life. They know one thing, **Jesus is going to use our faith and His testimony to win the battle for our souls to live with Him!**

The apostle Paul tells us, that while we are living here on earth, we see the future vaguely, but when Jesus comes again, we will see and understand it all! **So, as we live our lives here on earth, our faith goes on and on toward eternity with Jesus;** it is the very thing that carries us through! We have what I call "local faith" since we have our faith here on the earth, but our "lifetime faith" in Jesus Christ, and what He has in store for our future, is what true faith is all about!

Here in Revelation, the next event is **our** FAITH becoming a reality, our FAITH finally being realized, bringing us past the evil of this world to the glorious home that Jesus has been busy preparing for His people.

In this next event, FAITH is depicted as a white horse. The color white always depicts purity and righteousness in the Bible. Heaven opens to reveal a white horse, with a rider, called FAITHFUL (Trustworthy, Loyal, Incorruptible, steady) and TRUE. This rider passes judgment and wages war in righteousness. As we read Revelation's description of the rider, we realize that this rider is none other than Jesus Christ, Himself! **He is taking OUR faith and HIS testimony right out onto the battlefield to win the battle for ours souls!!!** His eyes blaze like a flame of fire, on His head are many crowns and He wears a title that only He knows the meaning of; but John tells us what it is!! He is called "THE WORD OF GOD" and He is dressed in a **blood-soaked robe.**

The troops of heaven, dressed in fine, dazzling white linen, ride out after Him. As they ride out to finish the war of all wars, He wields a sharp sword, and His inscribed title comes into full view, "KING OF KINGS AND LORD OF LORDS". **Here He comes to finish the battle for our souls,**

with our FAITH and His TESTIMONY!! He will smite the nations, and He will shepherd and control them with a rod of iron. He is not here to to be their king, He is here to round them up for slaughter! **It is now too late for anyone to change their mind and accept God's salvation.**

This is NOT a pretty sight!! I will warn you that it gets worse, even gruesome. The King of Kings is here to *"tread the winepress of the fierceness of the wrath and indignation of God the All-Ruler (the Almighty, the omnipotent)"*. As the King of Kings and His troops are descending upon the earth to finish the war, there comes a big announcement from heaven.

A single angel is stationed right in the light of the sun, and, in a huge mighty voice shouted to all the carrion-eating birds, *"Come gather yourselves together for the great supper of God, that you might feast on the flesh of generals and captains, the flesh of horses and their riders, and the flesh of all humanity, both slave and free, both small and great."* Who are all these people about to be horridly slaughtered and devoured?? They are everyone left on earth who persisted in their rebellious ways and followed the beast. These are the ones who refused to repent and follow Jesus, the very same ones who have been left "holding the bag" when Babylon was destroyed. These are virtually ALL of the remaining unsaved people in the world.

The beast is still around! He still has plenty of people in his ballpark, left over from the sudden destruction of Babylon. They were left hanging around just long enough to witness the amazing end of the beast and the false prophet! The beast gathers up all the remaining leaders and rulers of the earth to wage war on the rider of the white horse and His troops. No sooner had he gathered them all together, than he realized they were gathered there to face their doom!!

The beast was seized and overpowered, as was the false prophet who had performed wonders and miracles to deceive the people into following the beast and taking his tattoo, his mark of identity. Both of them were hurled into the fiery lake that burns and blazes with brimstone. The people who had followed them were killed with the sword that comes out of the mouth of Him Who rides the white horse. **The sword of Truth has slain their evil!**

The carnivorous birds were ready! They ate ravenously and gorged themselves on their dead bodies! I told you it wasn't pretty! Destruction and retribution are never pretty, but it is justified and necessary to eliminate evil so God's Plan for us can culminate. Our FAITH in Jesus Christ has made it happen!! **Our FAITH in Him is what has made it possible for Him to finish the war for our souls.** There are NO unsaved people left on the earth; the earth has been cleansed of all evil!! Hallelujah!

Satan Is Bound For 1,000 Years

Jesus Christ has taken down Satan's evil kingdom, thrown the beast and the false prophet into the lake of fire, the heavenly army has slaughtered all those who followed and worshipped them, and the vultures have devoured their flesh. Satan has lost everything and is standing here with his "bare face hanging out", with no one to support him; all his power to hurt people is gone. **Satan is alone and helpless!**

One powerful angel descended from heaven holding the key to the great Abyss, and holding a huge thick chain in his hands. This very strong angel grabbed and overpowered Satan single-handed and bound him with the chain. **The angel rendered him helpless! He then hurled him into the great Abyss, known as the bottomless pit, and closed it and sealed it shut above him.** Now he can no longer lead people astray, or seduce and deceive the nations, for a thousand years.

Right after John witnesses Satan being bound and shut in the Abyss, he is allowed to see what is going on for the thousand years Satan is confined to the Abyss and is prevented from deceiving anyone; the world is completely rid of him for a thousand years!

Everyone who has accepted Jesus Christ as their Savior will live and rule with Him now. John saw thrones, with people sitting on them, who had been given authority to judge and pass sentence (make decisions). John also saw all the people that had been martyred for witnessing and testifying about the Word of God, the Gospel. He saw all those who had refused to worship the beast and take his mark, plus all those who were spiritually whole, innocent and virtuous, virtually ALL who have become a new creature in Christ and have put Him first in their lives while on the earth. These are all the people being saved from the "second death", which is the permanent separation from God for all of eternity. These are the ones living and ruling with Jesus Christ for a thousand years here on earth.

Satan Is Released For A Short Time

After the thousand years, Satan will be released for a short time. Because Satan's sentence is final, with no chance for his repentance even after a thousand years, he is still bent on his old program of deceiving the people of the world! He's got new, virgin ground now; everyone is a potential victim! The world is now filled with a vast number of people who have never experienced Satan's evil ways, nor has he been able to influence any of them.

On the other hand, the people who have lived here during the thousand years also have the same choices of right and wrong as we have now. Although Jesus is right here on earth, clearly visible to everyone, there are certainly those who have gone on about their business and not particularly followed Jesus. This is a whole new crop of people who have the same choices as we have had, the only difference is that they have not had Satan influencing them.

When Satan is released from the Abyss, after one thousand years of being confined, he immediately goes out among all the people of the world to literally pick up where he left off! That is, to seduce, deceive and lead astray all the nations of the world, known as Gog and Magog (meaning the ends of the earth), to gather them for a climactic war on Jerusalem, Jesus its ruler and all those who follow Him. Once again, Satan has deceived himself!! He thinks he may be able to gather enough troops to overcome Jesus' established kingdom. He gathered such a huge army that their number was vast and nearly endless! These are the people who have been living on the earth WITHOUT Satan's evil influence, up until now. They are the very same people who have been living on earth, along with Jesus and His followers who are ruling with Him in Jerusalem. They have been free to go and come at will, they have been free to pick and choose just like we do, but with the advantage of no evil influence. They have had a thousand years to make up their minds; they WILL be judged by their personal decision.

Satan is sure he has a flying chance to win, since he has gathered so many people! The people are duped into thinking Satan has made a miraculous "comeback" to win the battle for our souls! The same old malady of the "madding crowd" still exits!! The madding crowd just goes on following the crowd to "who knows where"! They look good and smell good, so they go on down the wide and lovely road to nowhere, not checking out to see if it is headed toward Father God!

This madding crowd, this vast throng, joins Satan in getting ready to take over Jerusalem to rule there instead of Him! They swarm up over the broad plain of the earth and encircle the fortress of God's people, and the beloved city of Jerusalem. Lo and behold!! To their surprise, they get an extremely rude and instant awakening!!!

Holy fire descended from heaven itself and consumed them, right on the spot, before they had time to make any moves at all!!! Immediately, all in an instant, Satan was hurled into the very same lake of fire where the beast and the false prophet had been thrown earlier. They will be tormented day and night forever and ever. **End of story for Satan and all the horrors he has caused and evil he has continuously done!! He will NEVER again have an opportunity to influence anyone! THIS IS HIS BITTER END.**

The Great White Throne Judgment Of God

There is one more event that has to take place before the God of the Universe is completely done doing away with ALL traces and residue of evil among His creation. All of those **unsaved** people of the earth that have already died, are still waiting for God's final judgment and sentence. They have not been rescued from the earth like Jesus earnestly desired.

Now that all believers have been redeemed and are safely home with God, all of the unsaved, who have died in their sins, must be judged. They have been alive and waiting in a place the Bible calls Hades, literally, "the place of those who died". All the unsaved of the earth that have died were gathered to stand before God's throne to be tried, judged and sentenced.

As all the unsaved dead stood before God's throne, the books were opened, along with the Book of Life. In Psalm 139, the psalmist explains how meticulously God has created each one of us inside our mother's womb. While you and I were growing inside our mother's safe womb, God, Himself, wrote the story of your life the way He intended for it to be, unique to only you. Sadly enough, the story He wrote for our lives doesn't always go the way He wrote it. But wait!! **Repentance of sins cleans up** our story book! Hallelujah! But, alas, the masses never repair the damage to their personal book God wrote for each of them. Repairing the damages caused by our own sins can happen only by repentance and accepting Jesus Christ as our Savior. If repentance never comes, we will take the consequences of God's final judgment; end of story.

God is ALWAYS clear about what He expects from us all. He always wants us to understand what is right and what is wrong so we have a fair chance to make the right choices that will, ultimately, bring us back to Him. As the final chapters of Revelation are revealed to John, Jesus wants us to **know in advance** WHO is and isn't going to participate in God's new and perfect world. Right now, all these sins and conditions can be repented of, before the end of time as we know it; that is WHY Jesus has come to John to reveal these things to us AHEAD OF TIME.

Revelation lists the losers of eternal life, those who will not end up with Jesus:

- Cowards
- Ignoble
- Contemptible
- Cravenly lacking in courage
- Cowardly submissive
- Unbelieving and faithless
- Depraved, defiled with abominations
- Murderers
- Lewd and adulterous
- Those who practice magic arts
- Idolaters
- ALL liars

This crowd, now standing in God's final courtroom, is the very last of the unsaved people of the earth. These are the ones from the list you just read. Their opportunity, to accept Jesus as their Savior, ended when their physical bodies died, and they are here now to receive their sentence. Hades (the place of disembodied existence) has given them up at God's command. They are receiving the same judgment as every other person who lived on the earth without repenting and accepting Jesus as Savior.

"And the dead were judged and sentenced by what they had done [their whole way of feeling and acting, their aims and endeavors] in accordance to what was recorded in the books...and all were tried and their cases determined by what they had done [according to their motives, aims and works]. And if anyone's name was not found recorded in The Book of Life, he was hurled into the lake of fire." Rev. 20:12, 13, 15

Now that ALL sin, ALL evil and all people who chose it, are gone forever, there is no need for Hades, because death will never again come upon mankind! To close the books forever, death and Hades are hurled into the lake of fire that is the second and final death (separation from God).

THE VICTORY IS NOW COMPLETE!! Our segment of time is over, ended. God's perfect world for us can now be completed and activated! We can live there in perfect peace and happiness!

The Alpha & Omega, The Beginning & The End

God has won the battle for your soul!! He reigns supreme!! Everything that has gotten in the way of God's saving grace is gone! He is the Alpha, the beginning, and He is the Omega, the end. He began our lives and He has fought a great battle to give us a chance to end with Him. Time has ended and is no more; eternity goes on without end.

The big day has come for God to present our new environment to us! Immediately, John saw a brand new heaven and earth, for the one we know and lived on has vanished, along with the sea. He saw a breath-taking sight of a new Jerusalem descending out of heaven, spectacularly adorned like a bride for her husband! John heard a mighty voice directly from the throne of God:

"See! The abode of God is with men, and He will live (encamp, tent) among them; and they shall be His people, and God shall

135

personally be with them and be their God. He will wipe away every tear from their eyes, and death shall be no more, neither shall there be anguish nor grief, nor pain anymore, for the old conditions and the former order of things have passed away. 'See! I make all things new.' Record this, for these sayings are faithful (accurate, incorruptible and trustworthy) and true (genuine). 'It is done! I am the Alpha and the Omega, the Beginning and the End. To the thirsty I (Myself) will give water without price from the fountain of the Water of Life. He who is victorious shall inherit all these things and I will be God to him and he shall be My son.'"

Remember, that during all the phases of God's preparations to take down Satan, the Bride of Christ is in heaven preparing herself for the wedding feast. Now John has witnessed God's new world and the new Jerusalem descending from heaven adorned like a bride for her husband. One of the seven angels, who delivered the seven final plagues on earth, took John to show him the Bride, the Lamb's wife. John was taken in the Spirit to a huge and high mountain top and was shown the holy city of Jerusalem descending out of heaven from God.

The New Jerusalem And Its New World

God's world is brand new! It is free of all evil! It is now completely ready for all those who have been faithful to Jesus Christ. All things old and tainted have vanished! The victory has been won forever. Now God can bring in the new and perfect world.

The angel shows John the New Jerusalem, the Bride of the Lamb of God. It was clothed in God's stunning glory! It was brilliant like precious stones cut crystal clear. It had massive high walls with twelve gates, an angel stationed at each one. Each gate had the names of the twelve tribes of Israel inscribed on it. The walls had twelve foundation stones with the names of the twelve apostles of the Lamb inscribed on them.

The angel had a golden measuring rod to measure the city, along with the gates and walls. Lo and behold, the city is a huge square! Even more incredible, it is 1500 miles long, wide and tall!! What a city! The city, itself, is pure transparent gold! It's walls are Jasper. It's twelve foundation layers of the walls are: jasper, sapphire, chalcedony (white agate), emerald, onyx, sardius, chrysolite, jaccsinth, and amethyst. WOW! Can you imagine??

The twelve gates were twelve giant pearls, each being one giant pearl. The main street of the city was pure translucent gold. John didn't see a temple in the city, and soon discovered that the Omnipotent Lord God, Himself, and the Lamb, Himself, ARE the temple!

There is no need of a light source in the city, for the splendor and radiance of God illuminated it, and the Lamb is its Light; there is no night there in the city; it is light ALL the time. The city gates will never close. The nations shall walk in its light and bring their own glory into the city. They shall bring all their glory and majesty of their own nations to honor our Lord and King in the New Jerusalem. Now, God can allow the nations to flow through His kingdom because they are all righteous and good; there is no evil found in them (*Rev. 21:7*).

Now, the angel shows John the source of life eternal for all of us, the river that flows out of the very throne of God and the Lamb. It's waters sparkling like crystal, flowing down the middle of the broad way of the city, continually watering the Tree of Life. The Tree of Life produces twelve kinds of fruit, a fresh crop every month! Even its leaves have a vital purpose; the healing and restoration of the nations.

The light source in the New Jerusalem is God and Jesus Christ! There is no night or darkness there, no need for the sun because it is illuminated by the glorious presence of God, Himself! We will finally get to see the face of God and be in His presence, worshipping Him and serving Him forever and ever. In fact, His Name shall be on our foreheads and we will reign with Him as kings forever through the eternities of the eternities!

God's reconciliation with His creation is now complete!

Jesus Concludes His Revelation & Invitation To Mankind

"I, Jesus, have sent My messenger (angel) to give you reassurance of these things for the churches (assemblies). I am the Root (the Source) and the offspring of David, the radiant and brilliant Morning Star.

The Spirit and the Bride (the church, the true believers) say, 'Come!' And let him who is listening say, 'Come!' And let everyone who is thirsty [who is painfully conscious of his need of those things by which the soul is refreshed, supported and strengthened]; and whoever [earnestly] desires to do it, let him come, appropriate, and drink of the water of life without cost."

Rev. 22:16,17

The Angel Validates The
Truth Of Jesus' Revelation

"And he [of the seven angels further] said to me, 'These statements are reliable (worthy of confidence) and genuine (true). And the Lord, the God of the spirits of the prophets, has sent His messenger (angel) to make known and exhibit to His servants what must soon come to pass.'

(Jesus says), 'Behold, I am coming speedily. Blessed is he who observes and lays to heart and keeps the truths of the prophecy (the predictions, consolations, and warnings) contained in this book'" Rev. 22:6,7

The book of Revelation has been given to us by Jesus Christ, in person, to John for us so that we can have confidence in living our lives FOR Him, anticipating spending eternity with Him in a new world without any evil influence ever again. It is written specifically for you and me. We must have proof that the war for our souls will be totally won by Him!

The angel's last instructions for John is this:

"...Do not seal up the words of the prophecy of this book and make no secret of them, for the time when things are brought to a crisis, and the fulfillment is near." Revelation 22:10

Looking To Heaven Our Eternal Home

Your Own Personal Invitation From Jesus

My Beloved.

I want to invite you come into My kingdom and live in My world forever. All who have cleansed their garments and are thirsty for the water of Life, and practiced the truths of God's message are invited to live in My presence. My Father and I invite you to return and be with us.

We invite you to come drink of the waters of Life everlasting that is flowing from the throne of God. Come eat of the Tree of Life whose leaves are for your continual healing.

Come live in the New Jerusalem where you can see God and be with Me, worshipping freely. Come to a place free of pain and tears. Come join your loved ones and the millions that will be there.

I, Jesus, loved you enough to leave My beautiful home and come to earth to be like you, feel what you feel, go through the temptations, disappointments and harm that you go through. I personally know how you feel. I allowed God to abandon Me long enough to die on the cross and come alive again, taking all your sins away, to make a way for you to be saved from eternal death.

My invitation to you is good only until the end of time. After that, it will be too late, for time will be no more. You see, time is a metered segment of eternity; when the meter runs out, there will be no more time. I want you to be with Me! You must decide to accept My invitation while you are still alive on this earth. Your soul will not die with your body, but will go to the place you have chosen.

Now that I have come and chosen John to write the story of how it all will end, you can make an educated decision, knowing for sure that we will be victorious over ALL evil that has ever been.

Please accept My invitation, please accept heaven's invitation and come drink of the waters of eternal life.

I love you,
Jesus

A Warning To The Reader
Of Revelation

John concludes the script of Revelation with a warning to its readers from Jesus Christ, Himself. God does not want any part of the story left out, and He does not want any embellishments to it. It is extremely important for it to stay in its original presentation, as it reflects exactly what God is going to do to bring evil to a permanent end for all of us.

Jesus, personally, gives this warning in Revelation 22:18-20:

"I [personally, solemnly] warn everyone who listens to the statement of the prophecy the predictions and consolations and admonitions pertaining to them]in this book; if anyone shall add anything to them, God will add and lay upon him the plagues (afflictions and calamities) that are described and recorded in this book.

And if anyone cancels or takes away from the statements of the book of this prophecy [these predictions relating to Christ's kingdom and its speedy triumph, together with the consolations and admonitions or warnings pertaining to them], God will take away from him his share in the Tree of Life and in the City of Holiness (purity and hallowedness) which are described and promised in this book."

"He Who gives the warning and affirms and testifies to these things says, 'Yes, it is true, I am coming quickly.' Amen. Yes, come Lord Jesus!"